D1385659

TOP
100
CHILDREN'S MEALS

TOP

100
CHILDREN'S MEALS

SAFEWAY/GOOD HOUSEKEEPING

Text and illustrations copyright © Ebury Press and the
National Magazine Company Ltd 1993

All rights reserved. No part of this publication may be
reproduced in any form or by any means without permission.

Published exclusively for
Safeway
6 Millington Road, Hayes, Middlesex UB3 4AY
by Ebury Press
A division of Random House
20 Vauxhall Bridge Road
London SW1V 2SA

First published 1993

Edited by Felicity Jackson and Barbara Croxford
Designed by Peartree Design Associates
Special photography by Ken Field
Food stylist Kerenza Harries
Photographic stylist Suzy Gittins

The paper in this book is acid-free

Typeset by Textype Typesetters, Cambridge
Printed in Italy

ISBN 0 09 182102 9

COOKERY NOTES

All spoon measures are level unless otherwise stated.

Size 2 eggs should be used except when otherwise stated.

Granulated sugar is used unless otherwise stated.

The oven should be preheated to the required
temperature unless otherwise stated.

CONTENTS

Foreword

TOP 100 CHILDREN'S MEALS is one of a popular new series of colourful and practical cookery books created for Safeway customers. It contains 100 *Good Housekeeping* recipes guaranteed to delight children of all ages.

The Good Housekeeping Institute is unique in the field of food and cookery, and every recipe has been created and double-tested in the Institute's famous kitchens, using readily available ingredients.

As well as appetising and nutritious everyday recipes for breakfasts, suppers and snacks, there are lots of fun ideas for birthday and hallowe'en parties, picnics and school lunchboxes.

Moyra Fraser

COOKERY EDITOR
GOOD HOUSEKEEPING

BREAKFASTS

Breakfast Nog

MAKES ABOUT 600 ml (20 fl oz)

300 ml (10 fl oz) whole milk
175 ml (6 fl oz) orange juice
3 × 15 ml tbs Greek-style natural yogurt
1 large ripe banana
soft dark brown sugar, to taste
freshly grated nutmeg, to serve

1. Place all the ingredients except the sugar and nutmeg in a blender or food processor. Blend for 2 minutes until frothy.
2. Add the sugar to taste. Blend again for a few seconds. Chill.
3. Sprinkle with grated nutmeg and serve.

COOK'S TIP This is a good substitute for a proper breakfast or lunch.

Cinnamon Toasts

SERVES 1

2 thick slices of bread
25 g (1 oz) butter, softened
2 × 15 ml tbs soft brown sugar
½ × 5 ml tsp ground cinnamon

1. Grill the bread on one side only.
2. Cream the butter, sugar and cinnamon together and spread on the untoasted side of the bread.
3. Grill until the mixture starts to melt. Cut into fingers and serve immediately.

Breakfast Nog and Cinnamon Toasts

WALNUT WAFFLES

MAKES 10

225 g (8 oz) plain flour, sifted
1 × 15 ml tbs baking powder
2 × 15 ml tbs caster sugar
1 × 5 ml tsp salt
1 × 5 ml tsp ground ginger
3 eggs, separated
300 ml (10 fl oz) milk
4 × 15 ml tbs butter, melted
50 g (2 oz) walnuts, chopped
oil for cooking

1. Put the flour, baking powder, sugar, salt and ginger in a mixing bowl. Whisk in the egg yolks, milk and melted butter. Add the walnuts.
2. Just before cooking, stiffly whisk the egg whites and gently fold into the batter.
3. Heat a little oil in an 8 × 10 cm (3 × 4 in) waffle iron. Spoon in a little batter and cook for about 1 minute on each side. Keep hot. Repeat until all the batter is used up. Serve hot.

PERFECT PORRIDGE WITH RASPBERRIES

SERVES 4

1.2 lt (2 pt) milk
115 g (4 oz) medium oatmeal
salt
335 g (12 oz) fresh raspberries
thick cream, to serve

1. Bring the milk to a rolling boil in a large saucepan and sprinkle on the oatmeal in a steady stream, stirring all the time. Add the oatmeal slowly or it will form lumps. Stir until boiling, then turn down the heat and simmer gently for 30 minutes, stirring frequently until a thick but pouring consistency is reached. Add salt to taste at this stage – no sooner or it will toughen the oatmeal.
2. Pour into a warm bowl or tureen and serve with the raspberries and cream.

COOK'S TIP Make this fresh on the day and serve at once. Soft brown sugar or clear honey may be added, although this would be frowned on in Scotland.

BREAKFAST CROWDIE

SERVES 4

225 ml (8 oz) Greek-style natural yogurt
grated rind of ½ lemon
1 × 15 ml tbs clear honey
75 g (3 oz) toasted crunchy cereal
225 g (8 oz) fresh raspberries

1. Mix together the yogurt, lemon rind and honey (Add more honey to taste if wished). Stir in the crunchy cereal.
2. Spoon half into a large glass serving dish. Place two-thirds of the raspberries in a layer on top, then cover with the remaining yogurt mixture.
3. Decorate with the remaining fruit. Cover and chill for about 15 minutes.

COOK'S TIP Any cereal can be used for this, but toasted varieties tend to be the best. Don't layer the mixture too far ahead or the cereal will become soft.

Perfect Porridge with Raspberries

The Energiser

SERVES 8

50 g (2 oz) blanched almonds
50 g (2 oz) unsalted peanuts
50 g (2 oz) sugared, chopped dates
115 g (4 oz) oat flakes
115 g (4 oz) wheat flakes
25 g (1 oz) dried milk powder
50 g (2 oz) demerara sugar
50 g (2 oz) sultanas
milk and natural yogurt, to serve

1. Roast the almonds and peanuts under a moderate grill; cool and chop.
2. Mix all ingredients together, then store in an air-tight container.
3. Serve with milk and natural yogurt.

COOK'S TIP This is an excellent snack to start the day or for anyone who's ravenous after school.

Apple Muesli

SERVES 4

4 × 15 ml tbs rolled oats or fine oatmeal
150 ml (5 fl oz) fruit juice
4 eating apples
4 × 15 ml tbs cream or top of the milk
1 × 15 ml tbs clear honey
a little brown sugar
50 g (2 oz) sultanas or raisins
a few chopped nuts, such as walnuts or almonds

1. Place the oats and fruit juice in a bowl and leave overnight.
2. The next day, grate the apples with their skins on, keep a little back for decoration. Mix the rest with the remaining ingredients except the nuts.
3. Put the muesli into glasses, top with some grated apple and sprinkle with chopped nuts.

Yogurt with Dried Fruit

SERVES 4

450 g (1 lb) dried fruit, such as apricots, prunes, figs, pears, apples or peaches
600 ml (20 fl oz) water
115-175 g (4-6 oz) demerara sugar
piece of lemon rind
natural yogurt, to serve

1. Choose just one fruit or make a dried fruit salad. Wash the fruit and soak it for several hours or overnight in the water.
2. Cook the fruit in this water, adding the sugar and lemon rind. Stew gently until tender. Serve cold with natural yogurt.

Exotic Fruit Bowl

SERVES 8

1 large Galia melon
2 ripe papayas
410 g can of lychees in syrup, drained, syrup reserved
juice and rind of 1 lime
25 g (1 oz) large coconut flakes, to serve (optional)

1. Halve the melon and papayas. Discard the seeds, then peel and cut the flesh into chunks and put in a glass bowl. Halve the lychees, then add to the other fruits with the syrup.
2. Stir in the lime juice. Cover the bowl of fruit.
3. Lightly toast the coconut and sprinkle over the fruit just before serving with the lime rind.

COOK'S TIP If possible, chill before serving to allow the flavours to mingle.

Exotic Fruit Bowl

CORN AND HAM SCRAMBLE

SERVES 4

6 eggs
4 × 15 ml tbs single cream
15 g (½ oz) butter
198 g can sweetcorn, drained
115 g (4 oz) ham, finely chopped
large pinch of freshly grated nutmeg
salt and pepper
4 slices of hot buttered toast, to accompany
fresh parsley sprigs, to garnish

1. Beat the eggs and cream well together. Pour into a frying pan. Add the butter, sweetcorn, ham, nutmeg and seasoning.
2. Scramble over a low heat until just set. Pile equal amounts on to buttered toast and garnish with parsley sprigs.

BAKED EGGS IN A CRUST

SERVES 2

2 large thick slices of white bread, from
    an uncut loaf, about 2.5 cm (1 in) thick
softened butter or polyunsaturated
    margarine, for spreading
2 eggs
salt and pepper
grated Cheddar cheese

1. Trim the crusts from the bread and neatly scoop out the inside of each slice of bread to leave a narrow shell.
2. Spread the bread shells all over with butter. Bake in the oven at 190°C/375°F/Gas Mark 5 for 10–12 minutes.
3. Drop an egg into each bread shell, season and sprinkle with grated cheese. Bake for a further 10–12 minutes or until the egg has just set and the crust is crisp.

BREAKFAST PILAFF

SERVES 6

3 × 15 ml tbs sunflower oil
115 g (4 oz) onion or shallots, skinned
    and chopped
2 large red peppers, seeded and cut
    into large cubes
400 g (14 oz) mixed-grain rice
25 g (1 oz) toasted sunflower seeds
1.2 lt (2 pt) vegetable stock or water
6 eggs
450 g (1 lb) low-fat pork sausages
12 large fresh basil leaves, shredded
salt and pepper
basil leaves, to garnish

1. Heat the oil in a large frying pan and cook the onion for about 5 minutes or until softened but not coloured. Stir in the peppers, rice, sunflower seeds and stock. Bring to the boil. Turn down the heat, cover and simmer for 35 minutes without removing the lid or stirring, until the rice is tender and the liquid is absorbed.
2. Boil the eggs for about 8 minutes. Drain and cool under cold running water. Peel when completely cold and store in cold water.
3. Prick the sausages with a fork and place under a moderate grill. Grill for about 10 minutes until cooked right through and well browned. Cool slightly and cut into thick slices. Cover and keep warm.
4. Quarter the eggs. When the rice is cooked, stir in the sausage and shredded basil, and season to taste. Finally, gently stir in the eggs, cover and return to the heat to warm through for about 5 minutes. Turn into a warm serving dish and garnish with basil leaves.

Breakfast Pilaff

PICNIC SAMOSAS
MAKES 12

225 g (8 oz) lean minced beef
115 g (4 oz) red pepper, seeded and
    finely chopped
25 g packet tandoori spice mix
4 × 15 ml tbs mayonnaise
¼ × 5 ml tsp garlic purée
213 g packet chilled puff pastry
1 egg, beaten

1. Mix together the minced beef, the red
pepper, the tandoori spice mix, the mayonnaise
and the garlic purée.
2. Roll out the pastry to a rectangle about
33 × 43 cm (13 × 17 in). Trim the edges. Cut
into twelve 10 cm (4 in) squares.
3. Lightly brush each square with beaten egg.
Place a heaped teaspoon of the filling on one
side of each square. Fold over to form a triangle
and seal the edges with a knife.
4. Place on a dampened baking tray, brush with
a little beaten egg and pierce the top of the
parcel to allow the steam to escape.
5. Bake in the oven at 200°C/400°F/Gas
Mark 6 for about 20 minutes or until well risen
and golden. Cover lightly if necessary. Cool on
a wire rack.

VARIATION Use onion in place of red
pepper, if liked.

COOK'S TIP Samosas make ideal picnic or
lunchbox food; they won't spill and are
substantial enough to satisfy the heartist
appetite.

Picnic Samosas (left)
Courgette, Potato and Cheese Soup (right)

Courgette, Potato and Cheese Soup

SERVES 6

25 g (1 oz) butter or margarine
450 g (1 lb) courgettes, trimmed and sliced
175 g (6 oz) potatoes, peeled and sliced
1.2 lt (2 pt) chicken stock
about 8 fresh basil leaves
115 g (4 oz) mature Cheddar cheese, cut into
   small pieces
salt and pepper

1. Melt the butter in a large saucepan, add the vegetables and sauté for 1-2 minutes before stirring in the stock and basil leaves. Bring to the boil, cover and simmer for 8-10 minutes, or until the vegetables are very tender.
2. Purée the soup with the cheese in a blender or food processor. Season and reheat before pouring into flasks.

West Country Slices

SERVES 4

225 g (8 oz) boneless rib end pork steaks
50 g (2 oz) Cheddar cheese, cut into small cubes
1 small Cox's apple, cored and diced
1 × 15 ml tbs mango chutney
1 small onion, skinned and finely chopped
pepper
1 egg
213 g packet chilled puff pastry

1. Put the pork in a food processor, fitted with a metal blade, and process until finely chopped. Transfer to a large bowl.
2. Add the cheese, apple, chutney and onion to the pork and season with pepper. Beat the egg, then add half to the mixture. Mix well together.

3. On a lightly floured surface, roll out the pastry to a square measuring 26 cm (10½ in).
4. Put the pork mixture, in a sausage shape, down the centre third of the pastry. Using a sharp knife, cut the sides of the pastry, diagonally, into 1 cm (½ in) strips.
5. Brush the edge of the pastry with the remaining egg. Tuck the ends in then fold the strips, alternatively from each side, over the filling. Place on a dampened baking tray and brush the pastry all over with the remaining egg to glaze.
6. Bake in the oven at 220°C/425°F/Gas Mark 7 for 15 minutes, then reduce the temperature to 180°C/350°F/Gas Mark 4 for a further 20 minutes until golden brown. Leave to cool.
7. When cold, cut into slices before wrapping in foil.

VARIATION Use 225 g (8 oz) pork sausagemeat instead of the pork steaks.

Smoked Mackerel Pittas

MAKES 8

335 g (12 oz) smoked mackerel fillets
2 × 15 ml tbs mayonnaise
2 × 15 ml tbs natural yogurt
1 × 5 ml tsp creamed horseradish
black pepper
8 small pitta breads
mixed salad leaves, shredded
¼ cucumber, cut into sticks

1. Skin the mackerel and flake gently with a fork into bite-sized pieces. Mix together the mayonnaise, yogurt and horseradish, then season with pepper. Stir into the mackerel.
2. Split each pitta along one side, spoon in shredded salad leaves and cucumber sticks, followed by the fish mixture.

West Country Slices

Finger Sandwiches

MAKES ABOUT 18

225 g (8 oz) cooked chicken, skinned and
    finely chopped
150 g (5 oz) low-fat soft cheese
3 salad onions or ¼ cucumber,
    finely chopped
salt and pepper
butter or margarine
1 small medium-sliced loaf, about 400 g (14 oz)

1. Mix the chicken with the soft cheese and salad onions or cucumber. Season to taste.
2. Butter the bread and sandwich the slices together with the filling. Cut each sandwich into three to make finger shapes.

Cheese and Egg Pinwheels

MAKES 24

2 hard-boiled eggs, finely chopped
50 g (2 oz) Cheddar cheese, grated
2-3 × 15 ml tbs salad cream
salt and pepper
1 small, unsliced, split-tin loaf, about 400 g (14 oz)
butter or margarine, for spreading
mustard and cress

1. Mix the hard-boiled eggs with the cheese and salad cream. Season.
2. Remove the crusts from the loaf, then cut the bread lengthways into six thin slices. (Chilling the loaf first will make the pinwheels easier to prepare.) Press slices with a rolling pin to flatten.
3. Butter each slice of bread, then spread thinly with the egg mixture. Sprinkle over a little cress. Roll up each slice from the longest edge. Cut into four.

Continental Sausage Salad

SERVES 2

175 g (6 oz) small new potatoes,
    washed or scraped
50 g (2 oz) frozen sweetcorn
4 frankfurter sausages
1 × 15 ml tbs reduced-calorie mayonnaise
5 cm (2 in) piece of cucumber
pepper

1. Put the potatoes in a saucepan, add enough boiling water just to cover, then with the lid on, simmer for 15–20 minutes until tender. Four minutes before the end of the cooking time, add the sweetcorn. Increase the heat until simmering again, then continue cooking.
2. Meanwhile, cook the frankfurter sausages according to the instructions on the packet,then cut each sausage into five pieces.
3. When the potatoes and sweetcorn are cooked, drain well and put in a bowl. Add the mayonnaise whilst still warm and toss together. Add the sausages, then leave to cool.
4. Roughly dice the cucumber and add to the salad. Season with pepper. Mix together, then pack in individual plastic containers.

Omelette Rolls

SERVES 4

8 eggs
salt and pepper
4 × 15 ml tbs water
butter, for cooking
chopped mixed fresh herbs (optional)

1. Lightly whisk the eggs with the seasoning and water.
2. Heat a little butter in a 25 cm (10 in) non-stick frying pan. Add a small ladle of the egg mixture and swirl around the pan to give a thin

Omelette Rolls

layer. Leave to set and brown for about 30 seconds.

3. Loosen around the edges, then turn out the omelette on to a sheet of greaseproof paper.

4. Cook all the omelettes similarly, adding some fresh herbs to the egg mixture, if wished. Stack up with greaseproof paper between each omelette. Cover and cool.

5. Once cool, roll the omelettes up with one or more of the suggested savoury fillings and slice thickly to serve.

FILLINGS

• Mix chopped, cooked chicken with roughly chopped watercress sprigs and a little mayonnaise. Season to taste with salt and freshly ground black pepper and Dijon mustard.

• Mix small peeled cooked prawns with garlic mayonnaise, chopped cucumber and a little grated lemon rind and strained lemon juice. Season to taste.

• Spread thinly sliced salami or ham over the omelettes. Top with a little soft cheese and some shredded salad leaves.

• Coarsely grate carrots and mix with a little coarsely grated fennel and grated celery sticks. Add a dash of natural yogurt with lemon juice and wholegrain mustard and plenty of chopped parsley. Mix in grated Cheddar or Lancashire cheese to taste.

• Roughly chop tomatoes and radishes and roll inside the omelettes with salad leaves and a dash of lemon mayonnaise or Greek-style natural yogurt.

• Flake smoked trout or mackerel fillet and mix with mayonnaise, a dash of lemon or lime juice and a generous quantity of creamed horseradish to taste. Add some finely chopped cucumber or a crisp eating apple.

21

SAVOURY CUSTARD PIES

MAKES 24

225 g (8 oz) plain flour, sifted
salt and pepper
115 g (4 oz) butter
2 eggs
225 ml (8 fl oz) semi-skimmed milk
2 salad onions, trimmed and chopped
100 g can tuna steak in brine, drained and flaked
2 small tomatoes, chopped
25 g (1 oz) Cheddar cheese, finely grated
2 slices of lean cooked ham, chopped

1. To make the pastry, put the flour and a pinch of salt in a bowl. Rub in the butter until the mixture resembles fine breadcrumbs. Add enough water to bind the mixture together. Knead lightly, then roll out on a floured surface.

2. Thoroughly grease two 12-hole bun tins. Cut out 7 cm (2¾ in) pastry rounds with a fluted cutter and press each round into the bun tin.

3. Mix the eggs with the milk in a jug. Put a little salad onion and flakes of tuna in eight of the pastry cases. Arrange pieces of tomato and sprinkle with cheese in another eight cases. Divide the chopped ham amongst the remaining cases. Carefully pour the custard mixture equally into the pastry cases.

Savoury Custard Pies

22

4. Bake in the oven at 200°C/400°F/Gas Mark 6 for 35 minutes or until the filling is just set and the pastry lightly browned. Leave to cool before packing in a plastic container.

VARIATION Vary the fillings to suit the preferences and ages of the children. Chopped cooked chicken, peas, mushrooms, crisp bacon, cooked vegetables and smoked mackerel all work well.

Cheese Scone Twists

MAKES ABOUT 14

450 g (1 lb) self-raising flour
2 × 5 ml tsp baking powder
pinch of salt
75 g (3 oz) butter
115 g (4 oz) mature Cheddar cheese,
   finely grated
about 300 ml (10 fl oz) milk

1. Sift the flour, baking powder and salt together into a bowl, then rub in the butter. Add half the cheese and bind the mixture with milk.
2. Roll out on a floured work surface to 1 cm (½ in) thick. Cut out rounds with an 8 cm (3 in) cutter and remove the centres using a 4 cm (1½ in) cutter.
3. Lightly knead the trimmings, including the 4 cm (1½ in) rounds, and roll out. Cut out more scone rounds with a hole until all the dough is used.
4. Twist each ring to form a figure of eight and place well apart on buttered baking trays.
5. Glaze the scones with milk and sprinkle over the remaining cheese.
6. Bake in the oven at 220°C/425°F/Gas Mark 7 for about 12 minutes until well risen and golden brown. Leave to cool before packing in a plastic container.

Scotch Eggs

SERVES 4

4 hard-boiled eggs, shelled
2 × 5 ml tsp seasoned flour
a few drops of Worcester sauce
225 g (8 oz) sausagemeat
1 egg, beaten
fresh breadcrumbs for coating
vegetable oil for deep-frying
green salad, to accompany

1. Dust the eggs with the seasoned flour.
2. Mix the Worcester sauce into the sausagemeat and divide it into four equal portions. Form each quarter into a flat cake and shape it around an egg, making it as even as possible to keep the egg a good shape; make sure there are no cracks in the sausagemeat.
3. Brush with beaten egg and roll in the breadcrumbs.
4. Heat the oil in a deep-fat fryer to a temperature of 160°C/325°F, gently lower the Scotch eggs into the oil and fry for 7-8 minutes. (As the sausagemeat is raw, the fat must not be too hot or the meat will not have time to cook.)
5. When they are golden brown on the outside, remove and drain on absorbent kitchen paper. Leave to cool.
6. Cut the eggs in half lengthways and serve with a green salad.

VARIATION Scotch eggs can also be served hot with tomato sauce.

SAUCY SAUSAGES

SERVES 6

2 × 15 ml tbs tomato ketchup
1 × 5 ml tsp mild mustard
6 skinless pork sausages, about 175 g (6 oz)
    total weight
butter or margarine for spreading
6 small bridge rolls

1. Mix the tomato ketchup and mustard together. Coat the sausages lightly with the mixture.
2. Place on a foil-lined grill pan and place under a moderate grill until brown and cooked through, turning frequently during cooking. Cool, then serve in buttered bridge rolls.

VARIATION Use hot-dog sausages instead of the skinless sausages, if preferred.

CHICKEN AND SAUSAGE KEBABS WITH PEANUT DIP

MAKES 4 KEBABS

1 chicken breast, skinned
8 mini frankfurters
2 × 5 ml tsp sunflower oil
1 small onion, skinned and finely chopped
2 × 15 ml tbs peanut butter
1 × 15 ml tbs tomato ketchup
pepper
1 × 15 ml tbs water
8 cherry tomatoes, halved if large

1. Using a sharp knife, cut the chicken into 2.5 cm (1 in) pieces. Thread the chicken and frankfurters alternately on to four wooden kebab skewers.

Saucy Sausages and Cheese and Ham Pizza

2. Brush the kebabs with half of the oil and cook under a moderate grill for 15-20 minutes until cooked, turning frequently.
3. To make the dip, heat the remaining oil in a non-stick saucepan. Add the onion and cook for 3-5 minutes until softened. Transfer to a blender or food processor and add the peanut butter, tomato ketchup, pepper and water. Process until smooth.
4. Leave the kebabs to cool, remove from skewers, add the tomatoes and then wrap in foil or pack in plastic containers. Pack the dip in individual plastic containers.

VARIATION These kebabs can also be served at home on their skewers, under parental supervision. Add the tomatoes after grilling. Serve hot with the dip and cooked corn on the cob cut into thick slices.

CHEESE AND HAM PIZZA

SERVES 6

180 g packet pizza base mix
1 × 5 ml tsp dried mixed herbs
salt and pepper
115 g (4 oz) Cheddar cheese, grated
3 × 15 ml tbs tomato ketchup
115 g (4 oz) sliced ham, roughly chopped
2 tomatoes, sliced

1. Make up the pizza mix according to the packet instructions, adding the herbs, a pinch of salt and 25 g (1 oz) cheese to the dough. Knead, then press into a 26 × 16 cm (10½ × 6½ in) shallow tin.
2. Spread the tomato ketchup over the base, then top with the ham and sliced tomatoes. Sprinkle the remaining cheese over the top. Season to taste.
3. Bake in the oven at 220°C/425°F/Gas Mark 7 for 12-15 minutes or until well risen. Allow to cool thoroughly, then cut into fingers.

Nutty Treats

MAKES 24

4 × 25 g peanut brittle bars
115 g (4 oz) caster sugar
150 g (5 oz) ground almonds
3 × 15 ml tbs cornflour
2 egg whites
icing sugar, to dust

1. Roughly crush the peanut bars in a strong bowl, using the end of a rolling pin. Mix with the caster sugar, almonds and cornflour.
2. Whisk the egg whites and stir enough into the mixture to give a firm, slightly sticky dough.
3. Dust your fingers with icing sugar and roll the mixture into 24 balls. Place on two baking trays lined with non-stick baking parchment.
4. Bake in the oven at 190°C/375°F/Gas Mark 5 for 15-18 minutes or until golden brown and craggy in appearance. Cool for 5 minutes, then transfer to a wire rack to cool completely. Dust with icing sugar to serve.
5. Store in an air-tight container for up to a week.

COOK'S TIP Nutty treats are similar to macaroons, but have an even more chewy centre.

Strawberry Buns

MAKES 12

115 g (4 oz) butter or margarine
225 g (8 oz) self-raising white flour, sifted
50 g (2 oz) caster sugar
5 × 15 ml tbs strawberry jam
1 egg

1. Rub the fat into the flour, until the mixture resembles breadcrumbs, then stir in the sugar.

Mix 3 × 15 ml tbs jam with the egg and add to the dry ingredients. Bind together with a fork.
2. Shape the dough into 12 balls, then place on greased baking trays, flatten slightly and make a small hole in the top of each. Fill the holes with the remaining strawberry jam.
3. Bake in the oven at 200°C/400°F/Gas Mark 6 for 10-15 minutes or until just firm to the touch and golden brown. Cool and store in an air-tight container for up to a week.

COOK'S TIP Any flavour of jam can be used in these moist, crumbly buns.

Banana Flapjacks

MAKES 12

115 g (4 oz) butter or margarine
75 g (3 oz) golden syrup
25 g (1 oz) demerara sugar
175 g (6 oz) rolled oats
25 g (1 oz) sultanas
1 small banana, about 115 g (4 oz),
    peeled and mashed

1. Heat the butter, syrup and sugar together until evenly blended. Stir in the oats, sultanas and mashed banana.
2. Place paper cases in a 12-hole bun tin; spoon the oat mixture evenly into paper cases.
3. Bake in the oven at 180°C/350°F/Gas Mark 4 for about 20 minutes or until just firm to the touch. Leave to cool, then store in an air-tight container for up to a week.

COOK'S TIP This chewy flapjack mixture is baked in paper cases for easy carrying.

Strawberry Buns and Banana Flapjacks

CHEESE AND EGG TOASTIES

SERVES 2

2 rashers of streaky bacon
75 g (3 oz) hard cheese, such as Cheddar or
    Red Leicester, grated
I egg, beaten
salt and pepper
I tomato, chopped (optional)
2 slices of wholemeal bread
butter or margarine for spreading

1. Grill the bacon, then snip into pieces. Put the cheese into a small bowl with the egg, seasoning, tomato, if using and bacon.
2. Toast bread on one side. Spread with butter. Divide the cheese mixture between the bread.
3. Place under a moderate grill and cook until golden. Serve immediately.

CHEESEY TOMATO RAREBIT

SERVES 2

I large beef tomato
freshly ground black pepper
175 g (6 oz) Cambazola (blue brie)
2 slices of Emmenthal cheese
50 g can anchovy fillets, drained
black olives, stoned (optional)
toasted muffins, to accompany (optional)

1. Cut the tomato into six thick slices. Arrange in two small round gratin dishes. Grind some pepper over, then warm under a hot grill.
2. Thinly slice the Cambazola with a wet knife.
3. Place a slice of Emmenthal over each dish of tomato. Top with sliced Cambazola.
4. Grill until the cheeses have melted; garnish with a few anchovies and olives, if using. Serve with toasted muffins, if liked.

Cheese and Egg Toasties

SALMON AND PRAWN KEDGEREE

SERVES 4

115 g (4 oz) fresh or frozen green beans, trimmed
salt and pepper
50 g (2 oz) smoked salmon
50 g (2 oz) butter or margarine
2 × 15 ml tbs water
450 g (1 lb) cooked white rice
175 g (6 oz) peeled cooked prawns
3 hard-boiled eggs, shelled and roughly chopped
2 × 15 ml tbs chopped fresh parsley
parsley sprigs, to garnish

1. Halve the beans if necessary. Cook in boiling salted water until just tender. Cut the salmon into strips.
2. Melt the butter with the water in a large frying pan. Add the rice and cook over medium heat, stirring frequently, for 2-3 minutes.
3. Add the salmon, prawns, eggs, beans and parsley with plenty of seasoning.
4. Continue to cook over a medium heat, stirring frequently, until thoroughly heated through. Garnish with parsley sprigs.

VARIATION Gravadlax, a Scandinavian delicacy of salmon marinated in salt, sugar, pepper and dill, can be used to replace the smoked salmon for a more piquant flavour. Alternatively, use a mixture of Gravadlax and smoked salmon.

EGG FRICASSEE

SERVES 4

6 eggs
200 ml (7 fl oz) milk
slice of carrot, onion, bay leaf, 6 peppercorns, for flavouring
25 g (1 oz) butter or margarine
2 × 15 ml tbs plain flour
142 ml pot soured cream
2 × 5 ml tsp chopped fresh tarragon or
½ × 5 ml tsp dried tarragon
salt and pepper
chopped fresh tarragon, to garnish
puff pastry triangles, to accompany

1. Boil the eggs gently for 10 minutes. Tap the shells and place in cold water.
2. Bring the milk just to the boil with the flavourings and leave to infuse for about 10 minute; strain.
3. Melt the butter in a small heavy-based pan. Remove from the heat, stir in the flour, milk, soured cream, tarragon and seasoning. Return to the heat, bring to the boil, stirring all the time, and simmer for about 5 minutes.
4. Shell the eggs, then halve; reserve the yolk from one. Slice the remaining eggs, add to the sauce and simmer, without stirring, for 2-3 minutes to warm through. Season.
5. Garnish with the reserved sieved egg yolk, and chopped tarragon and accompany with the pastry triangles.

Chicken and Sweetcorn Potato Cakes

MAKES 12

200 ml (7 fl oz) milk
2 eggs
115 g (4 oz) plain flour
salt and pepper
450 g (1 lb) potatoes, peeled and coarsely grated
225 g (8 oz) onions, skinned and thinly sliced
225 g (8 oz) cooked chicken, finely chopped
198 g can sweetcorn, drained
butter and vegetable oil for frying

1. Whisk the milk and eggs together, then beat in the flour and a pinch of salt until smooth. Chill in the refrigerator.

2. Blanch the potato and onion together in a pan of boiling salted water for 2–3 minutes. Drain well and press out as much liquid as possible.

3. Stir the chicken into the batter with the sweetcorn, potato and onion. Season to taste.

4. Heat a little butter and oil in a frying pan. Spoon heaped tablespoons of the mixture into the pan, flatten and fry for about 4 minutes on each side. Drain well on absorbent kitchen paper and keep warm, uncovered, in a low oven. Repeat until all the mixture is used. Serve hot.

Chicken and Sweetcorn Potato Cakes

POTATO LATKES

MAKES ABOUT 6

450 g (1 lb) floury potatoes, peeled and
    coarsely grated
1 small onion, skinned and coarsely grated
1 egg
4 × 5 ml tsp plain flour
salt and pepper
vegetable oil for frying

1. Squeeze out the excess moisture from the
potatoes and onion with a clean tea towel. Beat
the egg until frothy and mix into the potatoes
and onion, sifting over the flour and seasoning
at the same time.
2. Stir the mixture well. Heat the oil in a frying
pan. Drop spoonfuls of mixture into the hot
oil, and fry over a medium heat until the latkes
are crisp and golden on both sides and tender in
the middle. Drain well on absorbent kitchen
paper.

VARIATION These crisp little potato cakes
can be topped with anything savoury –
scrambled egg, slices of fried sausage or grilled
tomato and bacon, diced cooked ham and
sweetcorn, or baked beans and grated cheese.

FILLED CROISSANTS

MAKES 8

225 g (8 oz) frankfurters,
    kabanos sausages or similar
115 g (4 oz) sliced ham
8 croissants
300 ml (10 fl oz) Greek-style natural yogurt
2 × 15 ml tbs wholegrain mustard
salt and pepper

1. Slice the frankfurters or kabanos sausages
thinly. Cut the ham into strips.

2. Split the croissants in half. Warm in the oven
at 150°C/300°F/Gas Mark 2 for 10–15 minutes
or until warm.
3. Put the yogurt and mustard in a small pan.
Add the sausages and ham, and warm through
gently. Season to taste.
4. Spoon into the croissants and serve
immediately – the filling will separate if left to
stand for too long.

BAKED TUNA-STUFFED POTATOES

SERVES 4

4 large potatoes, scrubbed and pricked
200 g can tuna steaks in brine, drained and flaked
25 g (1 oz) butter
142 ml pot soured cream
1 × 15 ml tbs chopped chives
salt and pepper
115 g (4 oz) streaky bacon, chopped
cooked green beans or a green bean, kidney bean
    and chick-pea salad, to accompany

1. Bake the potatoes in the oven at 180°C/350°F/
Gas Mark 4 for 1½–2 hours until just tender.
2. Slice the potatoes in half and scoop out the
flesh, leaving a thin shell.
3. Mash the potato flesh, then stir in the tuna,
the butter, soured cream, chives and seasoning.
4. Spoon the tuna mixture back into the potato
shells and mark the surface with a knife.
5. Place the bacon on top of the potatoes.
6. Place the potatoes in a shallow ovenproof
dish and return to the oven at
220°C/425°F/Gas Mark 7 for 20–25 minutes.
Serve with freshly cooked green beans or a
green bean, kidney bean and chick-pea salad.

Baked Tuna-Stuffed Potatoes

15-Minute Fondue

SERVES 3-4

½ chicken stock cube
150 ml (5 fl oz) single cream
25 g (1 oz) butter or margarine
1 small onion, skinned and finely chopped
4 × 5 ml tsp plain flour
250 ml (9 fl oz) milk
150 g (5 oz) mature Cheddar cheese, grated
salt and pepper
French bread pieces or vegetable crudités,
    to accompany

1. Crumble the stock cube into the cream and heat gently, whisking, until dissolved.
2. Heat the butter in a saucepan and gently fry the onion until soft. Stir in the flour and cook, stirring for 1 minute without browning. Beat in the milk and bring the sauce slowly to the boil, stirring, until smooth.
3. Add the cream and cheese, then mix well. Bring quickly to the boil, then season. Turn into a warm flameproof dish or small fondue pot. Serve with a basket of crisp French bread pieces or vegetable crudités.

Junior Antipasto

Junior Antipasto

SERVES 2

1-2 hard-boiled eggs, shelled
2 fingers of Gruyère or Cheddar cheese
1 apple
2 thin slices of ham
4 thin slices of salami
2 pickled cucumbers
2 cherry tomatoes (optional)
bread croûtes
brown bread sandwiches, spread with yeast
   extract savoury spread, or small cheese-
   flavoured biscuits, to accompany

1. Halve or quarter the eggs. Cut the cheese into cubes. Divide the apple into eighths, discarding the core.
2. Arrange all the ingredients on two plates and let the children nibble with their fingers.

Macaroni Cheese

SERVES 4

225 g (8 oz) dried macaroni
salt and pepper
65 g (2½ oz) butter or margarine
4 × 15 ml tbs plain flour
900 ml (1½ pt) milk
pinch of freshly grated nutmeg or
   ½ × 5 ml tsp prepared mustard
225 g (8 oz) mature Cheddar cheese, grated
3 × 15 ml tbs fresh breadcrumbs

1. Cook the macaroni in a large saucepan of fast-boiling salted water for about 10 minutes until just tender. Drain well and keep warm.
2. Meanwhile, melt the butter in a saucepan, stir in the flour and cook gently for 1 minute. Remove the pan from the heat and gradually stir in the milk. Bring to the boil and continue to cook, stirring, until the sauce thickens.

Remove from the heat and add seasoning, nutmeg or mustard, 175 g (6 oz) of the cheese and the macaroni.
3. Pour into an ovenproof dish and sprinkle with the remaining cheese and the breadcrumbs.
4. Place on a baking tray and bake in the oven at 200°C /400°F/Gas Mark 6 for about 20 minutes until golden and bubbling, or brown under a hot grill.

Pasta with Tuna

SERVES 2

1 × 5 ml tsp olive oil
3 – 4 salad onions, sliced
1 garlic clove, skinned and finely chopped
   (optional)
227 g can chopped tomatoes
1 × 15 ml tbs tomato purée
50 g (2 oz) frozen sweetcorn
salt and pepper
50 – 115g (2 – 4 oz) pasta shapes, such as
   twists, bows or shells
100 g can tuna steaks in brine, drained and flaked
80 g drum grated Parmesan cheese, to serve

1. Heat the oil in a non-stick saucepan, add the onions and garlic, if using, and cook for 3-5 minutes until softened and lightly browned, stirring frequently.
2. Stir in the tomatoes with their juice, the tomato purée and the sweetcorn and season with pepper. Bring to the boil, then cover and simmer for 10 minutes.
3. Meanwhile, cook the pasta in plenty of salted boiling water until just tender.
4. Just before serving, add the tuna to the sauce and heat gently.
5. Drain the cooked pasta, spoon into two individual serving bowls and top with the sauce. Serve with the drum of Parmesan cheese and let the children help themselves.

BALLS OF FIRE

MAKES 24

2 × 180 g packets pizza base mix
½ × 440 g jar tomato sauce
chopped ham or chicken, crispy bacon, sausage,
    mushrooms, a few olives, sweetcorn, for topping
grated Cheddar cheese

1. Make up the pizza mix according to the packet instructions. Divide it into small balls, some the size of walnuts, others the size of ping-pong balls and some slightly larger. You should make about 24 balls.

2. Flatten each ball with the palm of your hand, or use a rolling pin. Using scissors, snip all the way around the piece to give the fire ball effect. Place on greased baking trays, cover with a clean tea towel and leave in a warm place to prove until doubled in size.

3. When the dough has doubled in size, spread with the tomato sauce and topping of your choice. Sprinkle with some grated cheese. Bake in the oven at 230°C/450°F/Gas Mark 8 for 10–15 minutes (depending on the size).

Balls of Fire

PANCAKES
MAKES 8

115 g (4 oz) plain flour
¼ × 5 ml tsp salt
1 egg
300 ml (10 fl oz) milk
butter for frying

1. Sift the flour and salt into a bowl, make a well in the centre and add the egg. Beat with a wooden spoon, adding the milk gradually until incorporated. Allow to stand for 30 minutes.
2. To make the pancakes, first heat a little butter in an 18 cm (7 in) heavy-based frying pan until very hot, running it round to coat the sides of the pan; pour off any surplus.
3. Ladle or pour in a little batter, rotating the pan at the same time, until enough batter is added to give a thin coating.
4. Cook until the pancake begins to curl around the edges, revealing a golden brown colour underneath. Ease a palette knife under the centre and flip over.
5. Fry the other side until golden, then place on to a warm plate and cover. Continue cooking pancakes until all the batter is used, adding a small knob of butter to the pan each time.
6. Fill as suggested below and right.

COUNTRY PANCAKES
SERVES 4

25 g (1 oz) butter
115 g (4 oz) mushrooms, wiped and chopped
4 large tomatoes, skinned and chopped
8 pancakes (see above)
300 ml (10 fl oz) cheese sauce (see right)
150 ml (5 fl oz) natural yogurt
25 g (1 oz) Lancashire cheese, crumbled

1. Heat the butter in a pan and fry the mushrooms and tomatoes. Fill the pancakes with this mixture. Roll or fold up and arrange in a shallow ovenproof dish.
2. Mix the cheese sauce with the yogurt, then pour over the pancakes.
3. Sprinkle with the cheese. Brown under a hot grill and serve immediately.

BACON AND MUSTARD PANCAKES
SERVES 4

50 g (2 oz) butter
2 onions, skinned and roughly chopped
175 g (6 oz) boiled bacon, finely chopped
225 g (8 oz) apple, peeled and cored
225 g (8 oz) frozen cut beans, cooked
1 × 15 ml tbs wholegrain mustard
2 × 15 ml tbs plain flour
300 ml (10 fl oz) milk
115 g (4 oz) Cheddar cheese, grated
salt and pepper
8 pancakes (see left)
chopped fresh parsley, to garnish

1. Melt 25 g (1 oz) of the butter in a frying pan and fry the onions until softened. Stir in the bacon, apple and beans and sauté for 2-3 minutes. Remove from the heat and stir in the mustard.
2. Melt the remaining butter in a pan, stir in the flour and cook gently for 1 minute, stirring. Remove the pan from the heat and gradually stir in the milk. Bring to the boil slowly and continue to cook, stirring, until the sauce thickens. Simmer for a futher 2-3 minutes. Add the cheese and seasoning.
3. Fill the pancakes with the bacon filling and roll or fold up. Place side by side in an oven-proof dish and spoon over the cheese sauce.
4. Heat in the oven at 180°C/350°F/Gas Mark 4 for 25-30 minutes. Serve the pancakes garnished with chopped parsley.

37

FISH FRITTO

SERVES 2

50 g (2 oz) self-raising flour
2 large pinches of bicarbonate of soda
pinch of salt
150 g (5 fl oz) water
225 g (8 oz) haddock or halibut fillets, skinned
sunflower oil for deep-frying
lemon juice or tomato sauce, to accompany

1. Sift the flour, bicarbonate of soda and salt into a bowl. Gradually add the water, stirring all the time to make a smooth, thick batter.
2. Remove any bones from the fish and cut into strips the size of a little finger.
3. Heat the oil in a deep-fat fryer. Dip six or eight pieces of fish into the batter, then drain off the excess. Deep-fry until golden. Drain well on absorbent kitchen paper while frying the remaining fish.
4. Serve the fish hot in cones of greaseproof paper. Squeeze over lemon juice to serve or accompany with a tomato sauce.

CRISPY BAKED FISH

SERVES 2

225 g (8 oz) thin fish fillets, skinned
sunflower oil
50 g (2 oz) dried breadcrumbs
salt and pepper
baked tomatoes and green beans, to accompany

1. Wash and dry the fish and cut it into serving pieces. Dip into the oil, then coat with crumbs.
2. Arrange in a single layer in an oiled shallow dish. Season.
3. Bake in the oven at 200°C/400°F/Gas Mark 6 for 12-15 minutes without turning or basting, until the fish is cooked. Serve with baked tomatoes and green beans.

FISH CRUMBLE

SERVES 2-3

115 g packet frozen spinach or 225 g (8 oz)
   fresh spinach
salt and black pepper
2 × 184 g packs frozen cod in parsley sauce
2 hard-boiled eggs, chopped
115 g (4 oz) cooked peeled prawns (optional)
50 g (2 oz) butter or margarine
75 g (3 oz) plain flour
75 g (3 oz) mild cheese, such as Lancashire
   or Cheshire, grated
25 g (1 oz) fresh breadcrumbs
sautéed mushrooms with onion and peas,
   to accompany

1. Put the frozen spinach in a heavy-based saucepan and thaw over a low heat, adding a little water if necessary to prevent it sticking. Alternatively, wash the fresh spinach thoroughly, remove the stalks; then cover and cook in a large saucepan, without using any additional water, until limp. Drain the spinach thoroughly, press between two plates to remove excess moisture. Roughly chop and place in a 1.2 lt (2 pt) ovenproof dish and season well with black pepper.
2. Remove the frozen cod in parsley sauce from the packs, then place on top. Add the eggs and prawns.
3. In a medium-sized bowl, rub or fork the butter into the flour until the mixture resembles breadcrumbs. Stir in the grated cheese, breadcrumbs, and seasoning. Sprinkle over the fish.
4. Cook in the oven at 200°C/400°F/Gas Mark 6 for about 45 minutes or until the topping is golden and the fish is cooked. (Cover with foil towards the end of the cooking time, if necessary.) Serve accompanied by sautéed mushrooms with onion and peas.

Fish Fritto

CHEESE AND TOMATO DIP WITH SAUSAGES

SERVES 8

40 g (1½ oz) butter
40 g (1½ oz) plain flour
300 ml (10 fl oz) milk
pinch of salt
pinch of cayenne pepper
115 g (4 oz) Cheddar cheese, grated
4 × 15 ml tbs tomato ketchup
450 g (1 lb) pork chipolata sausages, fried and cut in half
pineapple chunks, to serve

1. Melt butter in a pan, stir in flour and cook gently for 1 minute, stirring. Remove from heat and gradually stir in milk. Bring to the boil and continue to cook, stirring, for 1 minute. Remove from heat. Add salt, cayenne pepper, cheese and tomato ketchup. Stir until cheese has melted.
2. Serve as a dip for hot fried chipolata sausages and pineapple chunks.

JACK-IN-THE-BOX SAUSAGES

SERVES 2

6 rashers of streaky bacon
3 long thin frankfurter sausages
1 × 5 ml tsp lemon juice
1 × 5 ml tsp salad cream
2 × 15 ml tbs natural yogurt
2 medium carrots, peeled and coarsely grated
1 apple, coarsely grated
cress, to garnish

1. Halve the bacon. Cut each frankfurter into four and wrap in bacon, securing with wooden cocktail sticks.
2. Cook under a medium grill, turning once until the bacon is crisp.

3. Mix together the lemon juice, salad cream and yogurt to make a dressing.
4. Arrange the carrot and apple, topped with dressing, on two plates with the sausages. Garnish with cress.

SAUSAGE AND BEAN CASSEROLE

SERVES 4-6

2 × 15 ml tbs oil
450 g (1 lb) pork and herb sausages
225 g (8 oz) onion, skinned and sliced
225 g (8 oz) carrots, peeled and sliced
400 g can plum or chopped tomatoes
430 g can chick-peas, drained and rinsed
430 g can red kidney beans, drained and rinsed
1 × 15 ml tbs cornflour
350 ml (12 fl oz) stock
1 × 5 ml tsp Tabasco sauce
2 × 15 ml tbs tomato purée
salt and pepper
crusty bread, to accompany

1. Heat the oil in a medium flameproof casserole and brown the sausages evenly – about 5 minutes. Remove from the casserole and cut into two or three pieces.
2. Lower the heat. Add the onion and carrots. Cook, stirring, until beginning to soften.
3. Return sausages to the casserole, with tomatoes, chick-peas and red kidney beans. Blend the cornflour with a little stock, add to the casserole with the remainder of the stock, Tabasco sauce, tomato purée and seasoning. Stir.
4. Bring to the boil, cover and cook in the oven at 160°C/325°F/Gas Mark 3 for about 1 hour, longer if possible to increase the depth of flavour. Serve with lots of crusty bread to soak up the juices.

Jack-in-the-Box Sausages

Witches' 'Fingers'

SERVES 8

250 g (9 oz) plain flour
pinch of salt
4 eggs
600 ml (20 fl oz) half-fat milk
4 × 15 ml tbs vegetable oil
675 g (1½ lb) long thin chipolata sausages
tomato sauce, to serve

1. To make the batter, place the flour, salt, eggs and milk in a blender or food processor and blend until smooth. Cover and leave to stand for at least 30 minutes. This will swell the starch grains and give a lighter batter.
2. Heat the oil in a large roasting tin and add the sausages. Bake in the oven at 220°C/425°F/Gas Mark 7 for 5 minutes or until browning and the fat is very hot. If the fat is not sizzling hot, place the tin on the top of the cooker and heat until it is. (The pudding will not rise if the fat isn't hot enough.) Remove the sausages with kitchen tongs.
3. Stir the batter and pour into the tin. The batter should sizzle as soon as it hits the fat. Quickly arrange the sausages in fives to look like fingers in the batter.
4. Immediately return to the oven and bake for 40-45 minutes until the pudding has risen and is golden brown. Serve drizzled with tomato sauce.

Big Barbecue Burgers

SERVES 2

salt and pepper
225 g (8 oz) lean minced beef
2 × 15 ml tbs vegetable oil
2 × 15 ml tbs cider vinegar
1 × 15 ml tbs brown sugar
1 × 5 ml tsp prepared mustard
5 × 15 ml tbs tomato ketchup
2 × 15 ml tbs water
hamburger rolls and salad, to accompany

1. Season the mince and shape into two super-sized patties. Stir the rest of the ingredients together and spoon thickly over the burgers.
2. Cook under a moderate grill for 4-5 minutes on each side, brushing the burgers with marinade during and after grilling.
3. Serve on lightly toasted hamburger rolls with lettuce, sliced tomatoes, onion and relish.

Barbecue Cheeseburgers

SERVES 4

450 g (1 lb) lean minced beef
salt and pepper
50 g (2 oz) Gruyère cheese, grated
3 × 15 ml tbs barbecue sauce
toasted baps, pitta breads, onion rings,
    dill pickles and shredded lettuce,
    to accompany

1. Beat together the beef, seasoning and cheese. Shape into four large flat patties about 11 cm (4½ in) in diameter.
2. Brush the barbecue sauce over the burgers. Barbecue or grill for 4-5 minutes on each side. Serve on lightly toasted baps or pitta breads with onions rings, dill pickles and lettuce.

Witches' 'Fingers'

MEATBALLS IN MUSHROOM SAUCE

SERVES 4

450 g (1 lb) minced beef
50 g (2 oz) fresh white or brown breadcrumbs
    (1-2 slices bread)
50 g (2 oz) onion, skinned and finely chopped
salt and black pepper
50 g (2 oz) mature Cheddar cheese, grated
½ × 5 ml tsp mild made mustard
1 egg, beaten
plain flour
2 × 15 ml tbs oil
425 g can cream of mushroom soup
wholewheat spaghetti, to serve

1. Mix together the minced beef, breadcrumbs, onion, lots of seasoning, cheese and mustard. Bind with the beaten egg. (You can do this in a food processor but be careful not to overblend.)
2. Transfer the meat mixture to a lightly floured board. Using floured hands, divide into 16 and roll each piece into a ball.
3. Heat the oil in a frying pan and brown the meatballs in two batches. Remove from the pan and drain on absorbent kitchen paper.
4. Remove excess fat from the frying pan and wipe out with kitchen paper. Replace the meatballs, pour the soup over and season with black pepper only. Cover and simmer gently for about 20-30 minutes or until tender and cooked.
5. Serve over wholewheat spaghetti.

COOK'S TIP The meatballs can be prepared the night before and stored, covered, in the refrigerator.

SAVOURY PARCELS

SERVES 4

1 × 5 ml tsp sunflower oil
1 small onion, skinned and finely chopped
225 g (8 oz) minced lamb or beef
1 garlic clove, skinned and finely chopped
    (optional)
1 medium carrot, peeled and coarsely grated
½ × 5 ml tsp dried mixed herbs
pepper
400 g can chopped tomatoes
25 g (1 oz) butter or margarine
8 sheets filo pastry, measuring 23 × 30 cm
    (9 × 12 in), thawed if frozen

1. Heat the oil in a non-stick saucepan, add the onion and cook for 3-5 minutes until softened and beginning to brown.
2. Add the mince, and garlic if using, and cook for a further 5 minutes until browned all over, stirring frequently. Stir in the carrot and herbs and season with pepper.
3. Stir in tomatoes. Bring to the boil. Simmer for about 30 minutes until the meat is tender and the liquid has evaporated. Leave to cool.
4. Thirty minutes before serving, gently melt the butter. Brush one side of the pastry sheets with the butter then place one sheet on top of another (two sheets are needed for each parcel), buttered side up. Set the remaining butter aside.
5. Divide the cooled mince mixture into four and place in the centre of the pastry sheets. Gather up the corners of the pastry to make four parcels and seal the tops together by pressing firmly. Arrange on a non-stick baking tray. Brush with the remaining butter.
6. Bake in the oven at 200°C/400°F/Gas Mark 6 for 20 minutes until golden brown.

LAMB KEBABS

SERVES 4

3 × 15 ml tbs olive oil

1 × 15 ml tbs lemon juice

1 × 15 ml tbs chopped fresh rosemary

salt and pepper

1 garlic clove, skinned and crushed

675 g (1½ lb) boned leg of lamb, trimmed and
  cut into 2.5 cm (1 in) cubes

8 small tomatoes, halved

8 button mushrooms, wiped

bay leaves

4 small onions, skinned and quartered

1 sweetcorn cob, boiled and sliced

lermon wedges and fresh coriander, to garnish

1. Mix together the olive oil, lemon juice, rosemary, seasoning and garlic. Add the lamb and marinate for 2 hours (or preferably overnight).

2. Remove with a slotted spoon, reserving the marinade.

3. Thread eight skewers alternately with meat cubes, tomatoes, mushrooms, bay leaves, onions and slices of sweetcorn.

4. Brush with the marinade and cook under a low grill for 10–15 minutes, turning the kebabs about three times, until the meat is tender. Garnish and serve with boiled rice.

Lamb Kebabs

Beany Liver Casserole

SERVES 4

335 g (12 oz) lamb's liver, cut into 2.5 cm (1 in) cubes
25 g (1 oz) plain flour
25 g (1 oz) butter
1 onion, skinned and chopped
115 g (4 oz) mushrooms, wiped and sliced
430 g can red kidney beans
150 ml (5 fl oz) beef stock
150 ml (5 fl oz) milk
2 × 15 ml tbs tomato purée
1 × 5 ml tsp dried mixed herbs
salt and pepper
boiled rice, to accompany

1. Coat the liver with flour. Melt butter in a large saucepan and fry liver, onion and mushrooms until brown. Add the beans.
2. Add remaining ingredients and simmer for 20–25 minutes. Serve hot on a bed of rice.

Lamb Chops with Leeks and Lentils

SERVES 4

4 loin lamb chops, about 115g (4 oz) each
1 small onion, skinned and finely chopped
115 ml (4 fl oz) fresh orange juice
salt and pepper
1 × 15 ml tbs oil
450 g (1 lb) leeks, washed, trimmed and
    cut into 1 cm (½ in) slices
115 g (4 oz) split red lentils, boiled rapidly for
    10 minutes then drained
1 × 5 ml tsp paprika
300 ml (10 fl oz) lamb stock
fresh coriander, to garnish
steamed or boiled potatoes, to accompany

Lamb Chops with Leeks and Lentils

1. Trim chops of fat; place in a non-metallic dish. Sprinkle onion and orange juice over the lamb and season with pepper. Cover and refrigerate for at least 12 hours, turning once.
2. Lift the chops out of the marinade; pat dry on absorbent kitchen paper. Heat the oil in a medium-sized frying pan and brown the chops on both sides. Drain on kitchen paper.
3. Add the leeks, lentils and paprika to the pan and stir over a moderate heat for 1 minute. Place the chops on the lentils. Pour in the marinade and stock and bring to the boil.
4. Cover and simmer for 20 minutes or until the chops are cooked. Adjust the seasoning. Served garnished with coriander and accompanied by steamed or boiled potatoes.

Sweet and Sour Pork

SERVES 4

450 g (1 lb) pork tenderloin or boneless pork steaks
1 × 15 ml tbs oil
½ cucumber, cut into sticks
225 g (8 oz) button mushrooms, wiped and sliced
2 large red peppers, seeded and sliced
225 g can pineapple slices in juice, drained and
    cubed
½ × 350 g jar sweet and sour sauce
salt and pepper
boiled rice or egg noodles, to accompany

1. Trim the pork of any excess fat. Slice diagonally across the grain into strips about 5 × 0.6 cm (2 × ¼ in).
2. Heat the oil in a large frying pan and stir-fry the pork over a high heat, until almost tender – about 5 minutes.
3. Stir in the vegetables and fry for 1 minute. Add pineapple and stir-fry for 1 minute more.
4. Add the sauce. Mix well, adjust seasoning and continue to cook until bubbling. Serve immediately, with boiled rice or egg noodles.

STICKY CHICKEN

SERVES 2

2 × 15 ml tbs vegetable oil
1 × 15 ml tbs clear honey
1 × 15 ml tbs soy sauce
1 × 15 ml tbs tomato ketchup
6 chicken drumsticks
salt and pepper
pitta bread and tomato pieces, to accompany

1. Mix together the oil, honey, soy sauce and tomato ketchup, then use to baste the chicken.
2. Cook under a moderate grill, brushing with marinade, until chicken is browned outside and cooked through – about 15 minutes.
3. Season and serve with pitta and tomato.

MILD CHICKEN CURRY

SERVES 4

8 boneless chicken thighs or about 450 g (1 lb)
    boneless chicken pieces
2 × 15 ml tbs oil
225 g (8 oz) onion, skinned and sliced
1 garlic clove, skinned and crushed
2 × 15 ml tbs mild curry paste
400 g can chopped tomatoes
200 ml (7 fl oz) chicken stock
2 × 5 ml tsp tomato purée
salt and pepper
boiled rice, tomatoes, cucumber and mango
    chutney, to accompany

1. Cut chicken into large bite-sized pieces. Heat oil in a medium-sized flameproof casserole and fry chicken until golden. Remove from casserole.
2. Lower heat, add onion and garlic. Cook until soft but not coloured. Stir in curry paste. Cook for 1-2 minutes.
3. Replace chicken, add tomatoes, stock, tomato purée and seasoning. Bring to boil. Cover and simmer gently for 20-30 minutes or until chicken is tender.
4. Serve with boiled rice and accompaniments, such as sliced tomatoes, cucumber and mango chutney.

CHICKEN WITH RICE, SWEETCORN AND PEPPERS

SERVES 4

275 g (10 oz) brown rice
salt and pepper
2 × 15 ml tbs oil
25 g (1 oz) butter
6-8 chicken thighs, 4 chicken breasts or
    4 whole chicken legs
225 g (8 oz) onion, skinned and sliced
300 ml (10 fl oz) chicken stock
2 × 5 ml tsp tomato purée
1 green pepper, about 175 g (6 oz),
    seeded and sliced
198 g can sweetcorn kernels, drained
2 × 15 ml tbs chopped fresh parsley
25 g (1 oz) toasted salted peanuts

1. Cook rice in boiling salted water until tender – about 30 minutes. Drain.
2. Heat oil in a medium-sized flameproof casserole. Add butter and when foaming fry chicken until golden on both sides. Remove from pan.
3. Lower heat, add onion and cook gently until soft but not coloured. Stir in stock, tomato purée, seasoning and green pepper. Replace chicken in the casserole, cover and cook gently for about 20-30 minutes or until chicken is tender.
4. Stir rice and sweetcorn into the casserole. Cook over a medium heat until the juices have evaporated and the rice is thoroughly heated through, stirring occasionally. Adjust seasoning; sprinkle parsley and toasted peanuts.

Sticky Chicken

MAGIC CHOCOLATE PUDDING

SERVES 4-6

50 g (2 oz) butter or margarine
75 g (3 oz) caster sugar
2 eggs, separated
350 ml (12 fl oz) milk
40 g (1½ oz) self-raising flour
5 × 5 ml tsp cocoa powder
whipped cream and raspberries, to serve

1. Beat butter and sugar together until light and fluffy. Beat in the egg yolks and stir in the milk.
2. Sift flour and cocoa powder together, then beat in until evenly mixed. Whisk the egg whites until stiff and fold into the mixture. Pour into a greased 1lt (1 ¾ pt) ovenproof dish.
3. Bake in the oven at 180°C/350°F/Gas Mark 4 for 35–45 minutes until the top is set and spongy to the touch. This pudding will separate into a chocolate sauce layer with a sponge topping. Serve hot with cream and raspberries.

CHOCOLATE TRIFLE

SERVES 10

8 trifle sponges
150 ml (5 fl oz) orange juice
225 g (8 oz) plain chocolate, broken up
4 × 15 ml tbs milk
600 ml (20 fl oz) Greek-style natural yogurt
grated white chocolate, to decorate

1. Cut each trifle sponge into six pieces and place in a serving dish. Pour over the orange juice.
2. Stir plain chocolate in a bowl with the milk over a pan of simmering water, until melted.
3. Mix into the yogurt and spoon on to the trifle sponges. Refrigerate until required. Serve decorated with grated white chocolate.

Magic Chocolate Pudding

CREAMY CHOCOLATE PUDDING

SERVES 6

115 g (4 oz) plain flour
2 × 5 ml tsp baking powder
40 g (1½ oz) cocoa powder
150 g (5 oz) sugar
1 × 5 ml tsp vanilla flavouring
150 ml (5 fl oz) single cream
75 g (3 oz) demerara sugar
350 ml (12 fl oz) boiling water
ice cream, to serve

1. Sift the flour with the baking powder and
2 × 15 ml tbs of the cocoa into a bowl. Stir in
the sugar, vanilla flavouring and cream, then
beat until smooth. Spread the mixture into a
buttered 1.3 lt (2¼ pt) ovenproof dish.
2. Mix demerara sugar with remaining cocoa
and sprinkle it over the mixture in the dish.
3. Pour the boiling water all over the pudding.
Bake in the oven at 180°C/350°F/ Gas Mark 4
for about 50 minutes until risen and the sponge
mixture (which will have come to the top) feels
slightly firm to the touch.
4. Turn out and serve with ice cream.

COFFEE AND CHOCOLATE FUDGE PUDDING

SERVES 4

115 g (4 oz) soft margarine
225 g (8 oz) soft light brown sugar
2 eggs
75 g (3 oz) self-raising flour
2 × 15 ml tbs cocoa powder
25 g (1 oz) walnuts, roughly chopped
25 g (1 oz) hazelnuts, roughly chopped
1½ × 5 ml tsp instant coffee powder
150 ml (5 fl oz) warm water
Greek-style natural yogurt, to accompany

1. Place the margarine, 115 g (4 oz) of the sugar
and the eggs in a medium-sized bowl. Sift in
the flour with 1 × 15 ml tbs of the cocoa. Beat
with an electric mixer until smooth and shiny –
about 2 minutes. Place in a 1.2 lt (2 pt) shallow
ovenproof dish, then smooth the surface with a
spatula.
2. Mix together the remaining cocoa, nuts and
50 g (2 oz) sugar. Sprinkle over the cake
mixture.
3. Dissolve the coffee powder in the warm
water. Add the remaining sugar, stirring to
dissolve. Pour the liquid over the mixture.
4. Bake in the oven at 180°C/350°F/Gas
Mark 4 for 40-45 minutes or until the pudding
is well risen and firm to the touch. (This
pudding separates as it bakes to give a delicious
fudgy sauce underneath a soft sponge.) Serve
hot with Greek-style natural yogurt.

PLUM AND MINCEMEAT PIE

SERVES 4-6

350 g packet frozen shortcrust pastry, thawed
4 × 15 ml tbs mincemeat
565 g can red plums, drained
egg white and caster sugar, for glazing
custard, to accompany

1. Roll out two-thirds of the pastry and use to
line a 21 cm (8½ in) pie plate – about 600 ml
(20 fl oz) capacity. Moisten the edges with
water.
2. Spread the mincemeat over the base. Top
with the plums.
3. Roll out the remaining pastry, carefully place
over the pie to form the lid. Seal and crimp the
edges.
4. Brush with lightly beaten egg white and a
sprinkling of caster sugar.
5. Bake in the oven at 200°C/400°F/Gas Mark
6 for 25-30 minutes or until the pastry is crisp
and golden. Serve warm with custard.

Plum and Mincemeat Pie

APPLE AND OAT CRUMBLE

SERVES 4

150 g (5 oz) butter or margarine
900 g (2 lb) cooking apples, peeled, cored and
roughly chopped
grated rind of 1 lemon
50 g (2 oz) raisins
1 × 15 ml tbs granulated sugar
115 g (4 oz) self-raising wholemeal flour
75 g (3 oz) porridge oats
50 g (2 oz) soft light brown sugar
25 g (1 oz) desiccated coconut
custard or ice cream, to accompany

1. Melt 25 g (1 oz) of the butter in a medium saucepan. Add the apples, grated lemon rind and raisins. Cover and cook gently, stirring occasionally until the apples have softened – about 10-15 minutes. Stir in the granulated sugar.
2. Mix together the flour, oats, brown sugar and coconut. Melt the remaining butter. Add to the dry ingredients and stir to mix.
3. Place the apple mixture into a 1.2 lt (2 pt) ovenproof dish. Top with the crumble mixture.
4. Bake in the oven at 190°C/375°F/Gas Mark 5 for 25-30 minutes or until golden. Serve hot or cold with custard or ice cream.

Raspberry Crunch Pie

SERVES 6

10 digestive biscuits
25 g (1 oz) chopped walnuts
75 g (3 oz) unsalted butter, melted
150 ml (5 fl oz) double cream
218 g can condensed milk
2 large lemons
225 g (8 oz) fresh raspberries
mint leaves or coarsely grated chocolate and
   icing sugar, to decorate

1. Crush the biscuits evenly but not too finely.
Stir in the walnuts and butter.
2. Press the biscuit mixture over the base and
up the sides of a 20 cm (8 in) loose-based fluted
flan tin. Bake in the oven at 190°C/375°F/Gas
Mark 5 for about 5 minutes. Leave to cool.
3. Whip the cream until it starts to hold its
shape. Lightly beat in the condensed milk,
grated rind of one lemon and juice of both.
4. Arrange the raspberries over the biscuit base
– reserve six. Press to level, but do not squash.
Swirl the lemon filling across the fruit. Chill in
the freezer for 30 minutes only. Cut into six
wedges, decorate each one with mint or
chocolate, reserved raspberries and icing sugar.

Pear and Orange Crunch

SERVES 4

2 × 415 g cans pear halves in natural
   juice, drained
grated rind of 1 lemon
3 large oranges
40 g (1½ oz) butter or margarine
3 × 15 ml tbs golden syrup
175 g (6 oz) porridge oats
75 g (3 oz) soft dark brown sugar
1 × 5 ml tsp ground mixed spice
Greek-style natural yogurt, to accompany

1. Cut each pear half into two and place half of
them in a 1.2 lt (2 pt) ovenproof serving dish.
Add the grated lemon rind.
2. Holding the oranges over the dish of pears to
catch any juices, cut away the skins. Slice the
oranges thickly and cut into quarters. Layer up
with the remaining pears.
3. Melt the butter and syrup in a medium
saucepan, add the oats, sugar and spice, stirring
to mix. Spoon the mixture over the fruits and
roughly level off the surface.
4. Bake in the oven at 180°C/350°F/Gas
Mark 4 for about 40 minutes or until the top is
crisp. Serve hot or cold with Greek-style
natural yogurt.

Strawberry Babas

SERVES 6

1½ × 5 ml tsp active dried yeast
3 × 15 ml tbs tepid milk
2 eggs, lightly beaten
50 g (2 oz) butter, melted and cooled
115 g (4 oz) plain flour
1 × 15 ml tbs caster sugar
25 g (1 oz) desiccated coconut
6 × 15 ml tbs redcurrant jelly or sieved
   strawberry jam
5 × 15 ml tbs lemon juice
450 g (1 lb) strawberries, hulled
soured cream, to serve

1. Lightly oil six 9 cm (3½ in) ring tins and turn
them upside down on absorbent kitchen paper
to drain off the excess oil.
2. Sprinkle the yeast on to the milk and leave in
a warm place for 15 minutes or until frothy.
Gradually beat the eggs and butter into the
yeast liquid.
3. Mix the flour, sugar and coconut together in
a bowl. With a wooden spoon, gradually stir in
the yeast mixture to form a thick smooth batter.
Beat together.

Strawberry Babas

4. Divide the yeast batter between the ring tins and cover with oiled clingfilm. Leave to rise in a warm place until the ring tins are nearly two-thirds full.

5. Bake in the oven at 190°C/375°F/Gas Mark 5 for 15-20 minutes until golden. Turn out on to a wire rack placed over a large plate.

6. Put the jelly and lemon juice into a small pan over a low heat. When the jelly has melted, spoon it over the babas until well glazed, allowing any excess to collect on the plate under the wire rack. Transfer the babas to individual serving plates.

7. Return the excess jelly mixture to the pan and add the strawberries; stir to coat. Remove from heat and cool for 15-20 minutes or until almost set. Spoon into the centre of the babas. Serve warm or cold with soured cream.

CHOCOLATE CHIP ICE CREAM WITH CHOCOLATE SAUCE

SERVES 8

750 ml tub low-calorie chocolate ice cream
75 g (3 oz) chocolate chip and nut cookies
4 × 15 ml tbs low-fat drinking chocolate powder
2 × 5 ml tsp arrowroot
100 ml (4 fl oz) skimmed milk
150 ml (5 fl oz) cold water

1. Soften the chocolate ice cream slightly at room temperature. Roughly crush the biscuits and fold into the softened ice cream. Spoon back in the container and refreeze.

2. Place the drinking chocolate powder and arrowroot in a small saucepan and blend with the milk and cold water. Heat gently, stirring continually, bring to the boil and simmer for 30 seconds only, allow to cool slightly.

3. Serve the ice cream with the warm chocolate sauce.

COOK'S TIP If you want to make this in advance, freeze the chocolate ice cream only. Make the sauce the day you want to eat it.

Chocolate Chip Ice Cream with Chocolate Sauce

STICKY PEAR UPSIDE-DOWN PUDDING

SERVES 6-8

PEAR LAYER:
75 g (3 oz) butter or margarine
115 g (4 oz) light brown soft sugar
2 × 415 g cans pear halves in juice

SPONGE:
225 g (8 oz) plain flour
175 g (6 oz) light brown soft sugar
1 × 5 ml tsp bicarbonate of soda
pinch of salt
2 × 5 ml tsp ground ginger
½ × 5 ml tsp grated nutmeg
3 × 5 ml tsp ground cinnamon
finely grated rind and juice of 1 large lemon
175 g (6 oz) black treacle
75 g (3 oz) butter or margarine
200 ml (7 fl oz) milk
2 eggs, beaten
custard, natural yogurt or cream, to serve

1. To make the pear layer, warm the butter and sugar together. Spoon into a 2.3–2.6 lt (4–4½ pt) shallow ovenproof dish. Drain the pears and arrange cut side down around the base of the dish.
2. To make the sponge, mix the flour, sugar, bicarbonate of soda, salt and spices together in a bowl. Add the finely grated lemon rind, then make a well in the centre of the dry ingredients.
3. Warm the treacle and butter together. When evenly blended, pour into the well with the milk and 3 × 15 ml tbs lemon juice. Add the eggs and beat well until evenly mixed.
4. Spoon the sponge mixture over the pears. Stand the dish on an edged baking tray.
5. Bake in the oven at 200°C/400°F/Gas Mark 6 for about 25 minutes. Reduce the oven temperature to 190°C/375°F/Gas Mark 5 and continue to cook for a further 50 minutes,
covering lightly if necessary. The pudding should be firm to the touch and a skewer inserted into the centre should come out clean.
6. Leave the pudding to stand for about 5 minutes. Run a blunt edged knife around the edge of the pudding. Invert on to an edged platter. Serve warm with custard, natural yogurt or single cream.

CINNAMON APPLE PANCAKES

SERVES 4

75 g (3 oz) butter
115 g (4 oz) fresh breadcrumbs
grated rind and juice of 1 lemon
675 g (1½ lb) cooking apples, peeled and sliced
50 g (2 oz) caster sugar
1 × 5 ml tsp ground cinnamon
8 pancakes (see page 37)
icing sugar, for dusting

1. Heat 50 g (2 oz) of the butter in a pan and fry the breadcrumbs until golden, stirring.
2. Place the remaining butter, lemon rind and juice, apples, sugar and cinnamon in a saucepan. Cover and cook to a purée, then add the breadcrumbs.
3. Divide the mixture between the pancakes and roll up. Place in an ovenproof dish and cover with foil. Heat in the oven at 180°C/350°F/Gas Mark 4 for about 25 minutes. Serve dusted with sifted icing sugar.

Strawberry Yogurt Whips

SERVES 4

142 g packet strawberry jelly tablet
2 × 15 ml tbs lemon juice
150 ml (5 fl oz) natural yogurt
225 g (8 oz) fresh strawberries

1. Break up the jelly into cubes and put in a heatproof measuring jug. Make up to 300 ml (10 fl oz) with boiling water. Stir until dissolved. Add the lemon juice and enough ice cubes to make up to 450 ml (16 fl oz). Stir until dissolved.
2. Pour half the jelly into a large bowl and put in the refrigerator until just beginning to set. Leave the remaining jelly in a warm place.
3. When the jelly in the refrigerator is just about to set, whisk vigorously then whisk in the yogurt.
4. Pour the mixture into four individual serving dishes and refrigerate until set.
5. Meanwhile, hull and slice the strawberries, reserving four whole strawberries to decorate.
6. When the whips have set, arrange the sliced strawberries on top, then spoon over the remaining liquid jelly.
7. Chill until set. Serve decorated with the reserved strawberries.

Marbled Apricot Fool

SERVES 4

225 g (8 oz) ready-to-eat dried apricots
shredded rind and juice of ½ orange
300 ml (10 fl oz) natural yogurt

1. Put the apricots in a saucepan and cover with water. Bring to the boil, then reduce the heat, cover and simmer for about 25 minutes until tender.
2. Drain the apricots well and leave to cool slightly. Put in a food processor or blender, add the orange juice and process to form a purée. Leave to cool.
3. Put alternate spoonfuls of the apricot purée and yogurt in four individual serving dishes, then gently draw them together with a knife to create a marbled effect.
4. Chill for 2-3 minutes before serving. Serve decorated with the shredded orange rind.

Jolly Lollies

MAKES 20

450 g (1 lb) plain dessert chocolate
10 large bananas
20 lolly sticks
hundreds and thousands
toasted desiccated coconut
Smarties or sugar flowers
grapefruit and oranges, to serve

1. Melt the chocolate in a bowl over a saucepan of simmering water.
2. Cut a banana in half widthways. Push a lolly stick into each of the cut ends to make two lollies from each banana.
3. Dip the banana halves into the chocolate. Use a pastry brush, if necessary, to brush the chocolate along the banana. It must be completely coated (don't forget the cut end). Place on a baking tray. Repeat until all the bananas are covered.
4. While the chocolate is still soft, sprinkle the bananas with hundreds and thousands, and desiccated coconut or decorate with a few Smarties or sugar flowers.
5. Once the chocolate has set, open freeze the lollies (still on the baking trays) then transfer to rigid containers, interleaved with greaseproof paper.
6. To serve, remove from the freezer about 10-15 minutes before eating. Cut a slice off the grapefruit and oranges so that they will stand flat and place each, cut side down, on a plate.

Using a sharp knife, make small cuts in the fruit skins. Push the lolly sticks into the cuts, so that the lollies stand up. Dot around the table.

VARIATION Almost any sweet can be stuck on to the chocolate to decorate, but don't use nuts, small children can choke on them.

COOK'S TIP Bananas will go black if frozen for any length of time, so make these lollies the evening before serving, no earlier.

Jolly Lollies

GINGERBREAD MEN

MAKES ABOUT 16

335 g (12 oz) plain flour
1 × 5 ml tsp bicarbonate of soda
2 × 5 ml tsp ground ginger
115 g (4 oz) butter, diced
175 g (6 oz) soft light brown sugar
4 × 15 ml tbs golden syrup
1 egg, beaten
currants, to decorate

1. Grease two or three baking trays. Sift the flour, bicarbonate of soda and ginger into a mixing bowl. Rub in the butter until the mixture resembles fine breadcrumbs, then stir in the sugar. Beat the syrup into the egg, then stir into the flour mixture. Mix together to make a smooth dough.
2. Knead the dough until smooth, then divide in half. Roll out, half at a time, on a floured surface until about 0.6 cm (¼ in) thick.
3. Using a gingerbread man cutter, cut out gingerbread men until all of the dough has been used, re-rolling and cutting the trimmings. Repeat with the second half of dough. Place the gingerbread men on the baking trays and decorate them with currants, to represent eyes and buttons.
4. Bake in the oven at 190°C/375°F/Gas Mark 5 for 12-15 minutes, until golden brown. Leave on the baking trays to cool slightly, then transfer carefully to wire racks and leave to cool completely. Store in an air-tight container.

Gingerbread Men

HARLEQUIN BISCUITS

MAKES 30

75 g (3 oz) plain flour
¼ × 5 ml tsp bicarbonate of soda
½ × 5 ml tsp ground ginger
25 g (1 oz) butter or block margarine
40 g (1½ oz) light soft brown sugar
1 × 15 ml tbs golden syrup
1 × size 5 egg, beaten
277 g packet ready-to-roll icing
icing sugar, to dust
liquid food colourings
juice of ½ small orange

1. Grease two large baking trays. Sift the flour, bicarbonate of soda and ginger into a bowl. Rub the fat into the flour and stir in the sugar. Add the syrup with enough egg to form a soft dough, then transfer to a lightly floured surface and knead until smooth.
2. Using a floured rolling pin, roll out the dough to a 25 cm (10 in) square. Cut into 2.5 cm (1 in) wide strips. Separate the strips then, cutting at an angle, cut off pieces to make diamond shapes.
3. Place the biscuits on the baking trays and bake in the oven at 190°C/375°F/Gas Mark 5 for 8-10 minutes until golden brown. Cool slightly then transfer to a wire rack.
4. When the biscuits are completely cold, roll out the icing on a surface dusted with icing sugar. Cut the icing into strips (as when making the biscuits). Paint each strip in multi-colours using food colouring. Wash and dry your brush between each colour. Cut off diamond shapes. Moisten the surface of each biscuit with a little orange juice and top each biscuit with a piece of icing. Leave to set. Store in an air-tight container.

Harlequin Biscuits

CHOCOLATE AND HONEY FUDGE FINGERS

MAKES ABOUT 12

225 g (8 oz) digestive wheatmeal or
  any plain biscuit
75 g (3 oz) raisins
50 g (2 oz) plain chocolate
2 × 15 ml tbs clear honey
75 g (3 oz) butter

1. Grease and base line an 18 cm (7 in) square tin. Roughly crumble the biscuits and add the raisins. Melt the chocolate, honey and butter together in a pan, then stir into the biscuit crumbs.
2. Mix thoroughly and press firmly into the prepared tin.
3. Freeze for 10 minutes or chill until firm, then cut into fingers. Store in the refrigerator.

PEANUT BUTTER COOKIES

MAKES 36

175 g (6 oz) butter
50 g (2 oz) peanut butter
115 g (4 oz) caster sugar
115 g (4 oz) soft brown sugar
1 egg
275 g (10 oz) plain flour
¼ × 5 ml tsp salt

1. Mix the butters, sugars and egg together in a bowl. Add the flour and salt and mix to a firm dough.
2. Make into 36 balls. Place on buttered baking trays and flatten with a fork, making a criss-cross pattern.
3. Bake in the oven at 190°C/375°F/Gas Mark 5 for 10-12 minutes until golden. Cool on trays. Store in an air-tight container.

ANIMAL BUTTER BISCUITS

MAKES ABOUT 12

225 g (8 oz) butter
115 g (4 oz) caster sugar
275 g (10 oz) plain flour
50 g (2 oz) fine semolina
about 24 currants
175 g (6 oz) icing sugar
about 1 × 15 ml tbs water
about 12 small apples, to decorate

1. Beat the butter well in a bowl, then gradually work in the sugar. Stir in the flour and semolina until well mixed, then knead.

2. Roll out on a lightly floured work surface, half at a time, to 0.6 cm (¼ in) thickness. Stamp out animal shapes. If the mixture sticks to the surface, roll out between pieces of non-stick baking parchment.

3. Lift the animals on to baking trays and press currants into the heads for eyes. Slide cocktail sticks into the bodies of the animals from the base.

4. Bake in the oven at 180°C/150°F/Gas Mark 4 for 15-20 minutes. Cool on wire racks.

5. Sift the icing sugar into a bowl. Stir in the water and mix until a smooth icing is formed. Using a fine nozzle, pipe the children's names across the animals with the icing. Make a small hole in the top of each apple and push in a biscuit on a stick.

COOK'S TIP This is a fun way of serving these biscuits for a children's party. If serving to very small children, make sure the cocktail sticks are removed before they are given the biscuits.

ICED MARZIPAN STARS

MAKES ABOUT 24

75 g (3 oz) butter
175 g (6 oz) plain white flour
75 g (3 oz) caster sugar
40 g (1½ oz) ground almonds
2 egg yolks
4 × 15 ml tbs apricot jam
115 g (4 oz) icing sugar, plus extra to dust
250 g packet marzipan
1 × 15 ml tbs coffee flavouring

1. Rub the fat into the flour until it resembles fine breadcrumbs. Stir in the caster sugar and ground almonds and bind to a dough with the egg yolks mixed with 1 × 15 ml tbs water. Knead lightly, then wrap in clingfilm and chill for 30 minutes.

2. On a well-floured surface, roll out half the dough at a time to a 0.3 cm (⅛ in) thickness and stamp out star-shaped biscuits; place on baking trays. Knead and re-roll the trimmings as necessary.

3. Bake in the oven at 180°C/350°F/Gas Mark 4 for 12-15 minutes until golden brown. Cool on a wire rack.

4. Warm the jam with 1 × 15 ml tbs water, sieve, then brush over one side of half the biscuits.

5. On a surface dusted lightly with icing sugar, thinly roll out the marzipan and stamp out star shapes. Place on the glazed biscuits, brush with apricot jam and place the remaining biscuits on top.

6. Mix the 115 g (4 oz) icing sugar with the coffee flavouring and 1 × 15 ml tbs water to give a soft icing. Pipe or drizzle over each biscuit. Store in single layers in air-tight containers for 4-5 days.

PILE OF MERINGUE BONES

MAKES ABOUT 16

2 egg whites, at room temperature
115 g (4 oz) caster sugar
cocoa powder, for dusting

1. With an electric hand beater, whisk the egg whites until stiff but not dry. Add the sugar, one teaspoon at a time, whisking until very stiff between each addition. The meringue should be very stiff and shiny.
2. Spoon into a piping bag fitted with a 1 cm (½ in) plain nozzle. Pipe on to non-stick baking parchment in rows. First pipe a finger about 8 cm (3 in) long. At each end, pipe two small blobs touching each other to form the nubs of the bones.
3. Bake in the oven at 140°C/275°F/Gas Mark 1 for about 1½ hours or until hard and dry. Remove from the baking parchment and cool on a wire rack. Pile the meringues on a plate and dust lightly with cocoa powder.

COOK'S TIP These fun meringues are perfect for a Hallowe'en or 'pirates' birthday party.

Pile of Meringue Bones

HEDGEHOGS AND LADYBIRDS

MAKES ABOUT 16

175 g (6 oz) butter
50 g (2 oz) caster sugar
I egg, beaten
50 g (2 oz) self-raising flour
3 × 15 ml tbs milk
225 g (8 oz) icing sugar
I × 15 ml tbs cocoa powder, dissolved in a
    little hot water
chocolate buttons and dolly mixtures,
    to decorate hedgehogs
175 g (6 oz) marzipan
red food colouring
dolly mixtures and Matchmakers,
    to decorate ladybirds

1. Beat 50 g (2 oz) butter and sugar together
until pale and fluffy. Gradually beat in the egg,
then fold in the flour and 1 × 15 ml tbs milk.
2. Divide the mixture between 16 well
buttered patty tins with rounded bases. Bake in
the oven at 180°C/350°F/Gas Mark 4 for about
15 minutes; cool on wire racks.
3. Meanwhile, make the chocolate butter
frosting. Sift the icing sugar into a bowl. Beat
the remaining butter until soft, then gradually
beat in the icing sugar. Add the cooled cocoa
mixture and enough of the remaining milk to
give a firm frosting.
4. For the hedgehogs, cover half the cold buns
with the chocolate frosting (reserving some for
the ladybirds), shaping to form a snout. Decorate
with halved chocolate buttons for the spines and
dolly mixture jellies for the eyes and snout.
5. For the ladybirds, colour the marzipan a deep
pink with red colouring, roll out thinly and use
to cover the remaining buns. Pipe lines and spots
on to the ladybirds with chocolate butter frosting
and use dolly mixtures for the eyes and pieces of
Matchmakers for the antennae.

CHOCOLATE BISCUIT CAKE

SERVES 8

115 g (4 oz) plain chocolate
I × 15 ml tbs golden syrup
115 g (4 oz) butter
2 × 15 ml tbs double cream
115 g (4 oz) digestive biscuits, broken up
25 g (I oz) raisins (optional)
25 g (I oz) glacé cherries, halved
50 g (2 oz) flaked almonds, toasted

1. Butter a loose-bottomed 15–18 cm (6–7 in)
cake tin or ring.
2. Break the chocolate into pieces and place in
a bowl over a pan of hot but not boiling water.
Add the syrup, butter and cream.
3. When the chocolate and butter have melted,
remove from the heat and mix well. Cool
slightly, then stir in the biscuits, fruit and nuts.
4. Turn the mixture into the prepared tin,
then lightly level the top. Chill for at least
1 hour before serving.

EXCEEDINGLY GOOEY CHOCOLATE BROWNIES

MAKES 24

565 g (1¼ lb) plain chocolate
225 (8 oz) butter, cut into pieces
3 eggs
2 × 15 ml tbs freshly made strong coffee
225 g (8 oz) caster sugar
75 g (3 oz) self-raising flour
½ × 5 ml tsp salt
175 g (6 oz) walnut halves, chopped
I × 5 ml tsp vanilla flavouring

1. Grease and line a baking tin measuring
21 × 29 cm (8½ × 11½ in) across the top and
19 × 26 cm (7½ × 10½ in) across the base.

Exceedingly Gooey Chocolate Brownies

2. Using a very sharp knife, roughly chop 225 g (8 oz) of the chocolate and keep on one side. Break the remaining chocolate into small pieces. Place the pieces in a heatproof bowl with the butter. Stand the bowl over a pan of simmering water and heat gently until the chocolate melts, stirring. Leave to cool.

3. Mix the eggs, coffee and sugar together in a bowl, then gradually beat in the chocolate mixture. Fold in the flour, salt, walnuts, vanilla flavouring and chopped chocolate. Pour the mixture into the prepared tin.

4. Bake in the oven at 190°C/375°F/Gas Mark 5 for 45 minutes or until just firm to the touch in the centre. Leave to cool in the tin.

5. When the cake is completely cold, turn out on to a board and cut into 24 squares.

CHOCOLATE FUDGE SLICE

MAKES 12

175 g (6 oz) butter
115 g (4 oz) digestive biscuits, crushed
115 g (4 oz) brown sugar
150 g (5 oz) plain flour
25 g (1 oz) cocoa powder, sifted
150 ml (5 fl oz) milk
fresh or canned fruit and cream, to serve

1. Melt 50 g (2 oz) of the butter in a saucepan. Stir in the biscuit crumbs. Press into a 20 cm (8 in) sandwich tin or flan dish and chill.
2. Beat together the remaining butter and sugar until smooth. Add the flour and cocoa. Stir in the milk and spread the mixture over the crumb base.
3. Bake in the oven at 190°C/375°F/Gas Mark 5 for 35-40 minutes. Allow to cool.
4. Serve with fresh or canned fruit and cream.

VARIATION Chocolate fudge slices can also be dusted with icing sugar and decorated with coffee-flavoured butter cream and hazelnuts.

KITTEN CAKES

MAKES 12

115 g (4 oz) butter
115 g (4 oz) caster sugar
2 eggs, beaten
115 g (4 oz) self-raising flour
175 g (6 oz) icing sugar
about 1 × 15 ml tbs water
Smarties, jelly diamonds and angelica, to decorate

1. Place paper cases in a 12-hole bun tin.
2. Beat the butter and caster sugar together until pale and fluffy. Add the eggs, a little at a time, beating well after each addition. Fold in the flour and divide mixture between the paper cases.

3. Bake in the oven at 190°C/375°F/Gas Mark 5 for about 20 minutes until golden and risen. Cool on a wire rack.
4. Sift the icing sugar into a bowl. Add the water and mix until a smooth icing is formed. Place a little icing on each cake and spread out to cover the tops.
5. To make the kitten faces, press Smarties into the icing for the eyes; halve the jelly diamonds for the ears; cut small pieces of angelica for the nose and whiskers.

RED NOSE BUNS

MAKES ABOUT 36

50 g (2 oz) soft margarine
50 g (2 oz) caster sugar
1 egg, beaten
50 g (2 oz) self-raising flour
¼ × 5 ml tsp baking powder
1 ripe banana, peeled and mashed
115 g (4 oz) icing sugar, sifted
about 1 × 15 ml tbs orange juice
red glacé cherries or red spherical sweets,
   to decorate

1. Put the margarine, sugar, egg, flour and baking powder in a food processor and process until smooth and well mixed. Add the banana and process for 1 minute.
2. Put a teaspoon of the mixture into about 36 small petits fours cases. Arrange the filled cases on a baking tray. Bake in the oven at 190°C/375°F/Gas Mark 5 for about 12-15 minutes or until golden. Cool on a wire rack.
3. When the buns are cold, make the glacé icing by mixing the icing sugar with the orange juice until smooth and just thick enough to coat the back of a spoon. Top each bun with a small blob of icing and stick half a cherry or a sweet on to each. Leave to set.

Red Nose Buns

CLOWN CAKE

SERVES 12-15

LARGE CAKE:
3 × 15 ml tbs cocoa powder
335 g (12 oz) self-raising flour
2 × 5 ml tsp baking powder
335 g (12 oz) caster sugar
335 g (12 oz) soft margarine
6 eggs
SMALL CAKE:
2 × 15 ml tbs cocoa powder
175 g (6 oz) self-raising flour
½ × 5 ml tsp baking powder
175 g (6 oz) caster sugar
175 g (6 oz) soft margarine
3 eggs
ICING AND DECORATION:
5 × 227 g packets ready-to-roll icing
red and yellow edible food colouring
coloured paper
liquorice catherine wheels and bootlaces, assorted
   sweets and 2 chocolate mini rolls

1. Grease 3 lt (5 pt) pudding basin and a 1.6 lt (2¾ pt) pudding basin. Line the bases with non-stick baking parchment.
2. To make the cakes (it's easier to mix one at a time), put all the ingredients in a food processor and process until smooth. Do not over process. Pour each one into its prepared basin and bake in the oven at 180°/350°F/Gas Mark 4 for about 1½ hours for the large cake, and 1 hour for the small cake, covering the tops of the cakes if they become too brown. Cool on wire racks.
3. To assemble the cake, trim the base of the large cake, if necessary, so that it stands level. Sit the larger cake, with the flat side down, on a board.
4. Hold the small cake upright in the palm of your hand. Using a sharp knife, trim around the wide top edge so that the cake curves inwards rather than outwards.

5. Colour one and a half packets of icing red, and one and a half packets yellow (or colours of your choice). Roll out the red icing and drape it over the large cake so that it covers half of it. Trim the icing around the base of the cake. Wrap the trimmings in greaseproof paper and set aside. Repeat with the yellow icing, covering the other half of the large cake. Neaten the join in the middle and press lightly together.
6. Cut a ruffle for the clown's neck from the coloured paper. Moisten the top of the large cake with a little water and arrange the ruffle on top. Press in lightly to stick in position.
7. Roll out the remaining packets of icing and use to cover the small cake. Trim the icing so that it is neat around the base. Reserve the trimmings as before. Smooth out any creases using firm rubbing movements. If the icing seems dry, moisten it with a little water.
8. Roll out the yellow icing trimmings and cut out star shapes with a small cutter. Stick on to the red icing. Unwind a liquorice catherine wheel and use to make stripes on the yellow icing. Stick a Smartie on to the middle of each star. Stick the sweets from the centre of the catherine wheels or other sweets of your choice, down the centre of the clown to represent buttons.
9. Roll a piece of the remaining red icing into a ball for the clown's nose. Rub it with your fingers until it shines. Stick it into position using a cocktail stick to secure it if necessary. Cut two short pieces of catherine wheel to make crosses for the eyes. Stick on to the cake with water. Make the mouth from a piece of yellow icing and a piece of liquorice.
10. Mould two oval shapes from the icing trimmings to represent hands. Push a satay stick into the sides of the cake where one arm should be. Push a chocolate mini roll on to the satay stick so that it goes all the way through the roll and sticks out just enough at the end to spear the clown's hand. Push the hand into position. Repeat, to make another arm, pushing the satay stick in at an angle so that this arm is raised. Cut

Clown Cake

two small ruffles from the coloured paper and attach one to each arm between the hand and the mini roll.

11. Cut lengths of liquorice boot laces and stick on to his head to make his hair (moisten the icing with a little water if necessary to make it stick.) Cover an upturned cake tin with coloured paper or kitchen foil and decorate with ribbon. Carefully transfer the clown on to the cake tin. Tie some inflated balloons on to his raised arm.

12. Cut a 23 cm (9 in) circle from a piece of coloured paper. Make a cut from one edge of the circle to the centre. Curve the paper round to make a hat. Secure with staples. Decorate the top with a pompom of shredded paper.

13. Remember to remove all sticks before serving the cake to the children.

CREEPY CAKE

SERVES 12-15

CAKE:
115 g (4 oz) cocoa powder, sifted
275 g (10 oz) light soft brown sugar
300 ml (10 fl oz) milk
115 g (4 oz) butter, softened
1 × 5 ml tsp vanilla flavouring
2 eggs
225 g (8 oz) plain flour, plus extra for dusting
1 × 15 ml tbs baking powder
CREEPY-CRAWLIES:
450-675 g (1-1½ lb) ready-to-roll fondant icing or
    white marzipan
assorted edible food colourings, including black,
    brown and yellow
a little glacé icing
liquorice bootlaces, jelly snakes etc
GREEN SLIME ICING:
450 g (1 lb) icing sugar
225 g (8 oz) butter
a few drops of almond flavouring
edible green food colouring

1. Grease a 1.8 lt (3 pt) ring mould. Dust with flour. To make the cake, put the cocoa and 150 g (5 oz) sugar into a medium saucepan with the milk. Slowly bring to the boil, whisking all the time until the mixture thickens and starts to bubble. Cool.
2. Cream the butter with the remaining sugar and the vanilla flavouring. Whisk the eggs, add to the creamed mixture a little at a time, beating well after each addition. Sift the flour with the baking powder and fold into the mixture. Beat in the cocoa mixture. If necessary add a little more milk; it should just pour.
3. Pour into the prepared mould and bake in the oven at 180°C/350°F/Gas Mark 4 for about 40-45 minutes or until risen and firm. Cool in the tin for 5 minutes then turn out on to a wire rack to cool completely.
4. Using 115 g (4 oz) of fondant icing, knead in

some brown food colouring and roll out to a thickness of 0.6 cm (¼ in). Cut out a circle to generously cover the hole in the centre of the cake. Use a saucer as a guide. This is to be the trap door. With a blunt knife mark lines to resemble planks of wood. Place on a baking tray lined with non-stick baking parchment and leave in a warm place to dry overnight.
5. Next day, paint the grooves with black or brown food colouring. Shape a ring for a handle and attach with a little glacé icing.
6. Using the remaining fondant icing or marzipan like modelling clay, make a selection of bats, spiders, worms and beetles, colouring the fondant accordingly. Use the liquorice to make spiders' legs and the jelly snakes for further decoration. Pipe eyes on to the creatures with icing, allow to dry, then paint on pupils with food colouring. Allow to dry overnight or longer.
7. When all the creatures have been made, make the icing. Sift the icing sugar into a bowl. Beat the butter until soft, then gradually beat in the icing sugar, adding a few drops of almond flavouring. Whisk in enough green food colouring to give the desired effect.
8. Place the cake on a board or plate and cover with the icing. Secure the trap door over the hole in the middle of the cake and prop open with a cocktail stick. Arrange the creatures over the cake, crawling all over and on to the plate. Make trails in the icing. Make sure that some creepies are crawling out of the trap door.

COOK'S TIP Serve this as the star attraction at a children's Hallowe'en party.

Creepy Cake

DRINKS

CURRANT COCKTAIL

SERVES 4-6

1 bottle sparkling mineral water
4 × 15 ml tbs blackcurrant fruit drink
1 × 5 ml tsp lemon juice
a few frozen fruits of the forest
fresh mint sprigs, to decorate

1. Pour the mineral water into a large glass jug. Add the blackcurrant fruit drink and the lemon juice and stir well. Place two or three frozen fruits of the forest in the bottom of each glass and pour in the currant cocktail. Decorate with a sprig of mint.

RASPBERRY MILK SHAKE

MAKES ABOUT 1.3 LT (2¼ PT)

225 g (8 oz) fresh or frozen raspberries
150 ml (5 fl oz) Greek-style natural yogurt
1 lt (1¾ pt) milk, well chilled
icing sugar, to taste
crushed ice, to serve

1. Place the raspberries in a blender or food processor and blend until quite smooth. Push through a nylon sieve to remove the pips.
2. Return the sieved raspberries to the blender. Add the yogurt and a little milk and blend until smooth. Add the remaining milk with a little icing sugar and blend again.
3. Check for sweetness, adding more sugar as necessary. Add the sugar very gradually as some children may prefer the milk shake unsweetened. Pour the milk shake into a jug with some crushed ice.

Left to right: Currant Cocktail, Two-Fruit Drink and Raspberry Milk Shake

SHAKES AND FLOATS

CHOCOLATE MILK SHAKE
Dissolve 1 × 15 ml tbs drinking chocolate in a little hot water. Cool. Stir in 300 ml (10 fl oz) cool fresh milk and place 1 × 15 ml tbs dairy vanilla ice cream on top of each shake. Serve with chocolate flake bars.
SERVES 2

STRAWBERRY MILK SHAKE
Follow the recipe for chocolate milk shake. Use 2 × 15 ml tbs strawberry jam instead of the drinking chocolate and omit the chocolate bars.
SERVES 2

NUTTY FRUIT MILK SHAKE
Put 300 ml (10 fl oz) cool fresh milk, 1 banana, peeled and sliced, and 150 ml (5 fl oz) hazelnut yogurt in a blender and switch on for 1 minute. Pour into chilled glasses, top with 2 × 15 ml tbs dairy vanilla ice cream and serve immediately.
SERVES 2

BANANA FLIP
Whisk together 300 ml (10 fl oz) cool fresh milk, 1 small banana, peeled and sliced and 1 × 15 ml tbs sugar until thick and frothy. Pour into chilled glasses over crushed ice, sprinkle with a little nutmeg and serve immediately.
SERVES 2

CHOCO MINT SHAKE
Put 600 ml (20 fl oz) cool fresh milk and 4-8 drops peppermint flavouring in a blender and switch on for 10 seconds. Add 4 × 15 ml tbs dairy chocolate ice cream and blend for a further 30-40 seconds until smooth. Pour into chilled glasses and sprinkle with 50 g (2 oz) grated chocolate. Serve immediately.
SERVES 4

MARASCHINO FLOAT
Put 115 g (4 oz) maraschino cherries with their syrup, 600 ml (20 fl oz) cool fresh milk and 4 × 15 ml tbs dairy vanilla ice cream in a blender and switch on for 25-30 seconds. Pour into chilled glasses, top each with a spoonful of dairy vanilla ice cream, decorate with a cherry and serve immediately.
SERVES 4

PINEAPPLE SHAKE
Put 300 ml (10 fl oz) cool fresh milk and 150 ml (5 fl oz) pineapple yogurt in a blender and switch on for 30 seconds. Pour into tall chilled glasses. Top with 4 × 15 ml tbs dairy vanilla ice cream, decorate with pieces of fresh pineapple and serve immediately.
SERVES 2

BITTER LEMON
MAKES ABOUT 900 ML (1½ PT)

2 lemons
600 ml (20 fl oz) water
115 g (4 oz) sugar
soda water, to serve (optional)

1. Cut the lemon into pieces, put in a saucepan with the water and bring to the boil.
2. Reduce the heat and simmer gently for 10-15 minutes until the fruit is soft.
3. Add the sugar and stir until dissolved.
4. Remove from the heat, cover and cool. Strain before using. Serve with soda water, if liked.

Pineapple Shake (left)
Chocolate Milk Shake (right)

Two-Fruit Drink

SERVES 2

2 small apples
300 ml (10 fl oz) fresh orange juice
115 ml (4 fl oz) soda water

Peel, quarter and core the apples. Blend until smooth with the orange juice. Divide between two glasses. Top up with soda water.

Still Lemonade

MAKES ABOUT 1.2 LT (2 PT)

3 lemons
175 g (6 oz) sugar
900 ml (1½ pt) boiling water

1. Remove the lemon rind thinly with a potato peeler.
2. Put the rind and sugar into a bowl or large jug and pour on the boiling water. Cover and leave to cool, stirring occasionally.
3. Add the juice of the lemons, strain and chill.

Citrus Punch

MAKES ABOUT 1.6 LT (2¾ PT)

juice of 2 grapefruits
juice of 2 lemons
juice of 5 oranges
150 ml (5 fl oz) pineapple juice
sugar, to taste
600 ml (20 fl oz) tonic water, chilled in the bottle
1 lemon, thinly sliced, to decorate

1. Strain the fruit juices into a bowl, mix well and chill.
2. Just before serving, add the sugar and tonic water. Decorate with lemon slices.

Pineapple Crush

MAKES ABOUT 1.5 LT (3 PT)

600 ml (20 fl oz) pineapple juice
juice of 1 orange
juice 1 lemon
sugar, to taste
1.2 lt (2 pt) ginger ale, chilled in the bottle

1. Combine the fruit juices, then sweeten to taste with sugar. Chill.
2. Just before serving, add the ginger ale.

Pine-Lime Sparkle

MAKES ABOUT 1 LT (1¾ PT)

600 ml (20 fl oz) pineapple juice
3 × 15 ml tbs lemon juice
150 ml (5 fl oz) lime juice cordial
50 g (2 oz) icing sugar
300 ml (10 fl oz) bitter lemon,
    chilled in the bottle
slices of lime (optional)

1. Put the pineapple and lemon juices and the lime cordial in a bowl and stir in the icing sugar. Chill.
2. Just before serving add the bitter lemon and some lime slices, if wished.

Quick Lemon Squash

SERVES 1

juice of ½ lemon
sugar, to taste
soda water

Put the lemon juice and sugar into a glass. Fill to the top with soda water.

ICE CREAM SODA

SERVES I

I glass soda water
I × 15 ml tbs vanilla ice cream

I. Whisk the soda water and ice cream together with a rotary whisk until frothy. Alternatively, blend at maximum speed for 1 minute in a blender or food processor.
2. Pour into a large glass and serve at once.

VARIATIONS

Grapefruit or Lime Soda Follow the above method and whisk together ½ glass soda water, 2 × 15 ml tbs grapefruit juice or 1 × 15 ml tbs lime juice and 1 × 15 ml tbs ice cream.

Ginger Soda Follow the method above and whisk together ¾ glass ginger beer, ¼ glass lemonade and 1 × 15 ml tbs ice cream.

ORANGEADE

MAKES ABOUT 900 ML (1½ PT)

2 oranges
I lemon
50 g (2 oz) sugar
600 ml (20 fl oz) boiling water

I. Thinly pare the orange rind, free of any pith. Squeeze the oranges and lemon, then strain the juice.
2. Put the rinds and sugar into a bowl and pour over the boiling water.
3. Leave to cool, stirring occasionally, then add the strained orange and lemon juice.

Pine-Lime Sparkle